AT THE FI

TRUE SOUTH AFRICAN STORIES

Roger Webster

The cover is by permission from The Lion Match Company Limited, the owner of the rights in the LION match box label.

Published by Spearhead
An Imprint of New Africa Books (Pty) Ltd.
99 Garfield Road
Claremont
7700

(021) 674 4136
nicholas.combrinck@dpp.co.za
fritz@dpp.co.za

First edition, third impression 2002

ISBN 0-86486-487-6

cover design by Toby Newsome
Design and typesetting by Peter Stuckey
Printed and bound by Interpak Books, Pietermaritzburg

Contents

Foreword

It was Patricia Glyn who first introduced SAfm Weekend producer, Bruce Whitfield, to the idea of Roger presenting a series of short stories, broadly entitled, 'Things they didn't teach you at school'. Bruce undertook the project enthusiastically – deftly handing it on to Jacqui Reeves when she took over the programme.

Fireside Chats was an immediate hit. It has become a much loved and talked about series. Each week Roger takes a 'pocket' of South Africa's past, and brings it to life in a way seldom done before. We have heard stories of magicians, shipwrecks, love found and love lost, ghosts and madness. He has touched on wars and cattle raids, justice and injustice and loyalty and betrayal. History was never like this at school.

He has breathed life into characters who until now lived only on the pages of textbooks and forgotten, dusty tomes in libraries around the country. He has fleshed out their personalities and provided an understanding of what motivated them. He has given them their rightful place in history, ensuring that they will not be forgotten. But Roger's mastery lies not just in the subject matter. His skill lies in the telling. They are 'stories' in the truest sense of the word – with all the drama and emotion that you would expect from a suspense novel or blockbuster movie. But they are true stories, not make-believe, though on occasion you would be forgiven for thinking otherwise.

I am not a political analyst, nor an anthropologist. I am a radio presenter. So who am I, really, to tell you what the value of history is? I am eminently under-qualified, having only obtained a 'C' for Matric History. But let me venture an opinion anyway. Roger reminds us that although life is transient, our past shapes our future almost as much as our present does. By hearing these stories on SAfm, now also published in this book, we can measure ourselves against both our past and our present. And, hopefully, we can move forward more confidently, and with greater moral strength to better manage what lies ahead. History is all about learning from our past and, while the history of our country may never be completely told, this book takes us one step closer.

And if all of that sounds too lofty to you – never mind. On these pages of real make-believe you will meet fascinating people and experience bizarre situations. This book is a supreme drama. Enjoy it from that perspective and, as an added bonus, you'll learn more about this country than you ever imagined possible.

Tony Lankester
Presenter: SAfm Weekend
September 2001

Fireside chats

This is a book containing stories of and for all South Africans. The stories are edited transcriptions of talks given over twenty months, by Roger Webster, on SAfm on Saturday mornings, under the rubric, 'Fireside Chats'.

They are all true stories of people and events that will continue to shape the future of our wonderful land.

After landing at the Cape, the Dutch wrote and recorded events from their point of view, to suit their particular needs. Then came the British and they recorded events with their own colonialist mind-set (ask any Xhosa in the Eastern Cape). Then came Union and the eventual rise of Afrikanderdom, with its own agenda.

So it is that from 1652 onwards, unbiased stories, and stories of foolishness, bravery, happiness and sadness, have seldom been told truly in our country. It is only since 1994 that we have been free to correct these many biased views. Here, for the first time, is an honest attempt to tell the wonderful stories of all our peoples which, we hope, will spread a healing balm on the terribly fractured psyche of our great Nation.

The story of Ernst Luchtenstein

Many men – soldiers, voortrekkers, trekboers, outlaws, etc. – for diverse reasons have chosen to disappear into the solitude of isolated places. One of the most interesting such stories that I have come across is that of Ernst Luchtenstein and the Karas Mountains of Namibia.

Ernst Luchtenstein's father was a transport rider, carrying supplies to the German army in the field during the war against the Hottentots. He later sent for his family. Frau Luchtenstein, along with Ernst, his two brothers and a sister, landed at Lüderitz bay in 1906. They travelled along the dusty road to Keetmanshoop in a convoy of seven ox-wagons, loaded with army provisions and the family's scant belongings.

Between the German outposts of Aus and Konkiep the train was intercepted by Cornelius, the feared leader of the Bethanie Nama. Ernst's mother, knowing that the country and its people were wild and wishing to preserve her family from certain death, ran up to Cornelius and knelt before him, begging him to spare them, but he told her to stand up. 'Kneel before God, but not before any man!' he said in perfect German.

The wagons were looted and all the military supplies taken, but not one thing was taken from the Luchtenstein wagon. There are so many tales of chivalry, of black men not harming women and children, particularly during the Frontier wars in the Eastern Cape – our history is full of them.

The family pressed onwards and met up with Ernst's father in

Keetmanshoop. Ernst stayed in school only a few months and then decided to go and work for his father as a 'touleier' (the leader of the team of oxen). He and his father soon fell out, however, and Ernst went to live with the Mackay family.

The Mackays were a different sort of family. Mackay had married a local Nama woman, and Ernst had the privilege of growing up with the Nama, learning to speak their language fluently and finding out about game tracking and all the lore of the veld, including how to gather veldkos and medicinal herbs and their uses. The Mackay farm was called Paradise and was situated 22 km north of Keetmanshoop.

In 1914 at the outbreak of the First World War Ernst was, of course, conscripted into the German army. Both his brothers were captured by the South African forces, but Ernst remained free until German South West Africa was surrendered to General Louis Botha in July 1915. Having lived as he pleased for so long, Ernst did not take to the idea of becoming a prisoner of war. He had heard that all the German soldiers were to be interned. As a matter of fact, he ranked as a reservist and would have been allowed to return to the farm, but he knew nothing of this.

A train loaded with South African troops was going south and as they wore only the semblance of a uniform, he tore off his German badges and shoulder-straps and, dressed in war-stained khaki, he passed as a member of the Commando. Just before Keetmanshoop he jumped train and vanished into the vast veld of South West Africa.

If you have ever seen the Karas Mountains, you would be able to imagine the wilderness Ernst sought refuge in, convinced that, if caught, he would lose his freedom and be interned as a prisoner of war. The summer rains of 1915 had been far more abundant than usual. The natural springs and fountains had revived and veldkos was everywhere. Owing to his upbringing in the Nama family, Mackay, Ernst was able to live off the land. At the outbreak of the war he had buried his rifle along with fifty rounds of ammunition, and this he took with him into the mountains. His worldly goods consisted of a field-grey army greatcoat, a spear, a few mess-tins, his rifle and ammunition, and a mongrel dog that had followed him into the mountains.

Ernst trained the dog to catch dassies and each day when the dassies came down to graze, the dog would pounce, so providing a regular meal for both of them. Often Ernst would make Nama-type snares for guinea fowl and partridge and when this failed, he would resort to the age-old Bushman trap, consisting of a flat stone supported by a stick and baited with seeds. That stone fell upon many a guinea fowl! Ernst had so much meat that he seldom used his rifle, but when he did, he made sure that he brought down a kudu or a gemsbok. He cured the skins and used the leather to make shoes and clothing.

After six months of avoiding all humans, he felt it was safe to make contact with the Nama in the area, who gave him milk and later a goat. For the meat-satiated Luchtenstein this was an absolute luxury!

Beginning to feel secure, he visited local farmers near the mountains, but after almost eighteen months he learned from the local Nama that the police were looking for him. He became more careful and decided to wander off across the great plains to the Karas Mountains, where the last of the Bondelswart clan had made their stand against the Germans, prolonging the war for a further two years. From these peaks Ernst could scan an enormous area – westwards was the old dry bed of the Fish River and in the north-west he could see the cone of the extinct volcano, Brukkaros. This vista covered hundreds of square kilometres, but never did he see any signs of pursuit. It lulled him into a false sense of security and one afternoon, while resting in his little hut, he heard the sound of horses' hooves. He knew the game was up.

Two police troopers entered the hut. They said they had been searching for him for a very long time and that an army Captain in Keetmanshoop wanted to see him urgently! Despondently, he accompanied them to Keetmanshoop, but when he was taken to see Captain Tilley, the officer said: 'I want to go hunting and everybody around here says that not only are you the best shot, but you also know where all the kudu are! Will you take me hunting please?' All the way to Keetmanshoop Ernst had been thinking miserably about being put behind bars, so he was staggered by this outcome. Naturally he accepted gratefully! After the shooting trip Tilley gave him a contract

3

to supply grass for army horse fodder and he made £2 000 in four months.

Finally, he was able to go farming, and the time he had spent in those mountains proved to be invaluable. He had come to know every hectare of ground there and, as land was cheap in those days, he purchased land where he knew it would rain. Later on, when the karakul sheep industry boomed, Ernst made a fortune. At one time he owned more than 400 000 ha – nearly 1 000 000 acres of land. However, a change in the land tax system forced him to reduce it to a mere 60 000 ha.

Later, he opened a general dealer's store in Keetmanshoop and used to fly to New York to buy goods. Often he would fly over the mountains and look down, reminiscing on how he had managed to survive and to succeed in becoming so wealthy.

Luchenstein's family and children have left Namibia now and are living in the Cape and the Northern Province. They contacted me after the story of their father was broadcast.

The Emperor of North America

This is the almost incredible story of an 1820 Settler who became 'Emperor of the United States of America and Protector of Mexico'.

The boy, Joshua Abraham Norton, destined to be Emperor, was only one year old when he arrived in Cape Town in the *Belle Alliance,* with his parents, John and Sarah Norton, and his brother Lewis. His father acquired a farm in the Albany District and also opened a general dealer's store in Grahamstown. His elder brother Lewis enjoyed the distinction of being a foundation pupil of SACS, that famous college opened in 1829 in Cape Town.

As a young man, Joshua worked in his father's shop in Grahamstown. When he was twenty-two years old, he decided to start his own business in Port Elizabeth. This enterprise was not successful and after struggling along for a couple of years, he became insolvent in 1844.

Joshua's father had in the meantime transferred to Cape Town, where he had established a chandlery business and a general store. He too was unsuccessful and died in 1848, just before he was to be declared bankrupt.

It was at this time that the rumours of the fabulous gold discoveries in California reached the Cape, and the young thirty-one year old Joshua, sickening of the hardship of his life at the Cape, decided to seek his fortune in the Californian gold rush of 1849.

He arrived just in time to qualify as a 'Forty-niner' and within a few years had made a considerable fortune as a commission agent. But a number of rash speculations, including an abortive attempt to corner the rice market, led to his being involved in lengthy litigation and his eventual bankruptcy. This must have been the final blow.

Encouraged by his friends, he now began to have delusions of grandeur and to talk about what he would do if he were Emperor of America. Out of this arose his belief that he was indeed Emperor.

The usual fate of a paranoiac is the lunatic asylum, but fate was exceedingly kind to Joshua Norton. When the aspirant Emperor put forward his claims to imperial rank and power, his friends treated this as a joke, while the great mass of his future 'subjects' remained completely uninvolved.

But fantastic things happened in the rough, pioneering days of that amazing mining camp – San Francisco. The public, already fed up with mob rule, scandalous rackets, street murders and public lynching, was now ready to welcome any new diversion. One of the newspapers, the *San Francisco Bulletin,* seized the opportunity and began to play up 'Emperor Norton'. In an astonishingly short space of time, the joke caught on, and the Emperor was established, first as a local and then as a regional figure and, finally, as a celebrity of international repute.

It all began when the *Bulletin* of 12 September 1859 published the first of his Imperial Edicts, that were soon to become such a feature in the life of the people of San Francisco. On that fateful day, the citizens opened their papers and read the following amazing notice:

At the peremptory request and desire of a large majority of the citizens of these United States, I, Joshua Norton, formerly of Algoa Bay, Cape of Good Hope, and now, for the last 9 years and 10 months past of San Francisco, declare and proclaim myself Emperor of these United States, and in virtue of the authority thereby in me vested, do hereby order and direct the representatives of the different States of the Union to assemble in the Music Hall of this City on the 1st day of February next, then and there to make such alterations in the existing laws of the Union as may be applicable under which the country is labouring, and thereby cause confidence to exist, both at home and abroad, in our stability and integrity.

Signed: Norton the First, 'Emperor of the United States'

At first this caused only a ripple of amusement throughout the country, but as edict followed edict in quick succession, the public began to rally to the support of their new ruler. Soon, he had a huge following of loyal, devoted subjects, and his regime became firmly enshrined in the hearts of the people. For the next twenty years, this kindly, lovable, eccentric, self-appointed despot, guided the destiny of his adopted country with a firm, patriarchal hand.

'Since he has worn the Imperial Purple', said a local San Franciscan newspaper, 'he has shed no blood, robbed nobody, and disposed the Country of no one'; and it is to his credit that, unlike so many other dictators, he lived and died a poor man.

The 'Imperial Palace' was a small, poorly furnished room in a third-rate boarding house. Here the Emperor would attire himself in the royal uniform – a gorgeous blue military affair with glittering brass buttons and huge gold braid epaulettes. It was actually the cast-off uniform of an army officer who had donated it to him. His sword of state hung down by his side and on his head was perched a tall white beaver hat, decorated with the plume of an eagle, peacock or rooster feather, held in place by a brass cockade. In his hand he held a heavy, twisted stick, which bore the inscription, 'Norton the First – Emperor of the United States'.

Dressed in his royal uniform, he would issue forth to receive the obeisance of his subjects and to collect the Imperial dues and, as even Emperors must live, he devised his own method of taxation. On the leading citizens of San Francisco he levied a tax of 50 cents a month. In return he issued his own promissory notes – 'Bonds of the Empire' they were called. These were valued at 50 cents, carried a 5% interest rate, and were payable in 1880.

When one or two of the bondholders were unscrupulous enough to present these in 1880, the Emperor was placed in a position of deep embarrassment, as the imperial coffers were empty. He solved the dilemma by accepting these bonds and issuing a new series in their place, payable in 1890!

Very rarely did any of his subjects refuse to pay up, but the Emperor did not need much, as the Imperial patronage was of such high advertisement value that exclusive restaurants were proud to entertain such royalty free of charge. The fashionable tailors made his uniforms for nothing. Leading railroads and at least one shipping company provided free transport when the Emperor felt inclined to travel. Moreover, his bond notes and proclamations were printed for him free of charge.

During his reign, Norton the First issued hundreds of proclamations by means of which he settled the affairs, not only of America, but the whole world. It is true, of course, that the telegrams that he so frequently despatched to his fellow rulers never got further than the wastepaper basket of the San Francisco Post Office, but he was unaware of this. Soon his subjects entered into the joke, and began to send him telegrams, which came ostensibly from famous people all over the world!

A sore point with Joshua was that, in spite of his proclamation as Emperor, the American Constitution still continued to function. This slight on his authority could not be overlooked, so he issued a number of fiats by which he abolished the House of Representatives, the Californian Supreme Court, the Republic of the USA, the President, the Vice-President and the Speaker of the House of Representatives, along with the Democratic and Republican parties.

In 1862, the Emperor, grieved at the suffering of the people during the Mexican Civil War, issued an edict annexing that country to his own realm and adding 'Protector of Mexico' to his title.

Inevitably, as reports of his wise and beneficial rule spread, many famous people 'wrote' to him for advice and guidance, among others Queen Victoria, Leon Gambetta, Abraham Lincoln, Jefferson Davis, the Emperor of China, Queen Isabella of Spain, Benjamin Disraeli and the Czar of Russia.

Quite early in his reign, the Emperor realised that it was his duty to marry a princess of royal blood and he received many advantageous offers. After much careful consideration he reduced the list to three. These highly honoured ladies were Princess Alice of England, the Queen of the Friendly Islands and Queen Victoria! But in his heart of hearts, Joshua had the greatest admiration for Victoria Regina and was firmly convinced that an alliance with her would cement the bonds of friendship between Britain and America. You can imagine his excitement when he received the following telegrams in quick succession:

Paris September 26th 1879
To: Norton the 1st Emperor of the United States and Protector of Mexico.

Through diplomatic circles, we understand that Queen Victoria will propose marriage to you as a means of uniting England and the United States.
Consider very much and do not accept. No good will come of it. Watch for letters.

Signed: Grevy, President of the French Republic.

The next one was even more impressive:

St. Petersburg, September 26th 1879

We are advised that Queen Victoria will join you in wedlock to bind closer ties between the United States and England. We approve most heartily and congratulate you.

Signed: Alexander II, Czar of Russia.

Unfortunately, there must have been a last-minute hitch, as Victoria Regina failed to offer her hand in marriage.

On the evening of 8 January 1880 the Emperor, still a bachelor, was walking to attend a meeting of the Hastings Debating Society when he slipped and fell. A loyal subject hurried to his assistance, but the Emperor was beyond human help. Within a few minutes he had passed away. Joshua Norton's body, clothed in a black satin robe, a white shirt and a black tie, lay in state at the San Francisco Coroner's office and, between 7 a,m, and 2 p,m, on the day of the funeral, 10 000 mourners,

9

representing every stratum of Californian society, passed the coffin to pay their last respects to their gentle, beloved sovereign.

Today, the remains of this one-time 1820 Settler lie in the beautiful setting of the Woodlawn Masonic Cemetery on the outskirts of San Francisco and over his grave stands a red marble tombstone bearing the simple inscription:

Norton the 1st
Emperor of the United States of America
And
Protector of Mexico

Joshua A. Norton
1819 to 1880.

Rachel de Beer

If on your way down the N3 towards Natal, you afford yourself the pleasure of stopping off at Van Reenen Village and visiting its historic Little Church and the lovely old wayside inn called the Green Lantern, owned by Lew and Maria, you will become acquainted with the area in which this story takes place.

Just to the north of the village runs the old road from the Transvaal to Port Natal, and the pass is known as De Beer's Pass. It is named after an old Freestater named Herman de Beer, who in the late 1870s owned a farm on top of that part of the Drakensberg between the Transvaal Republic and the Orange Free State.

One of the biggest dangers in the area is the cold. During the winter months, snowfalls are often accompanied by winds that drop the temperature so swiftly that even during the day animals have been known to freeze to death on those open plains.

One winter Herman de Beer was visited by a man of the same name, who was looking to buy a farm in that area. He was accompanied by his wife and two children, a boy of six or seven and a girl of twelve years named Rachel. They had a small number of stud cattle, along with some sheep and goats and, as there was an unoccupied hartbeeshuis on the farm, Herman offered to let them stay there, to afford the man a chance to look around for a farm.

Scarcely a week later, just after midday, a terrible storm came in from the south-east. Heavy dark clouds came rolling over the mountain peaks and the icy wind cut through the thickest clothing like a knife. The young animals from the summer lambing season had to be attended to immediately and everyone on the property, even old Herman, was busy carrying the young lambs into the barns, and herding the cattle into the kraals where they could huddle together to ward off the bitter cold. The younger De Beer was not rich and with his comparatively few cattle and sheep he could scarcely afford to lose any. When he had accounted for his herds, he noticed that a young cow, which had only just calved, was not accompanied by her new calf. As the herd had not been far from the house, it was easy to follow the spoor to locate the new calf. Night was falling fast, no time could be wasted and everyone had to help in the search. Rachel, or Raggie as she was called, was an energetic young girl who had grown up with cattle and already helped her father to take care of his herd. She often acted as herder and could milk cows, inspan a team of oxen and drive a wagon. So it was decided that the father, along with a Koranna assistant, would look further afield while Rachel searched the area nearest to the house.

Just before leaving, the young brother insisted on going with Rachel. It was bitterly cold, but these children were accustomed to a hard way of life and even their mother saw nothing wrong in the boy accompanying his elder sister. After all, it was close to the house and they wouldn't be away that long. So she wrapped him up warmly in a sheepskin kaross and the two of them went searching for the calf.

It is not necessary to drag out this tragic story. It was long after dark that the father and his Koranna servant returned, but Raggie and Boetie were still not back. The storm was vicious. The wind was so strong that it was difficult to keep one's direction, and the falling snow was turning to ice. The alarm was raised. The mother lit a big dung fire next to the house. The father, along with the Koranna and another two servants with lanterns, all heavily wrapped up in blankets, started the search for the children.

Throughout the night they searched, shouting, calling and shooting continually, but to no avail. At dawn the storm began to abate. The wind died down and the snow ceased to fall. At this stage the mother joined the search, but there was scant hope in anyone's heart. What shelter was there on those cold plains? The only possible hope was that they had found refuge in a deserted antbear hole.

Just after sunrise, one of the labourers picked up the spoor. The children had walked through the first and then the second dale and had evidently become completely lost in the storm and the darkness and, when the labourer signalled and the rest of the search party joined him, this is what they found.

A relatively big termite mound had been hollowed out with a sharp stone, to resemble the oven used by the trekkers. The mound might have been partly hollow when Raggie found it. She had made many such ovens for her own mother. Chipping away with a stone, in the bitter cold, with her little brother lying next to her almost unable to move, and slowly freezing to death, she had managed to make the excavation big enough for him to squeeze into.

It had long been dark when she had carried him over fifty metres to the termite mound. Her arms must have been almost paralysed when she started digging, but she worked without stopping, though slower and slower in the cold, until the hole was finished – and then she had made her final decision.

She was found naked, with only her small velskoens on her feet, curled around the entrance to the little cave she had dug, completely blocking it. She was dead, her body almost as white as the surrounding snow. Inside the ant heap was Boetjie, curled up tight and close to death, and over his clothes were those of Raggie – her dress, her petticoat and her thick sheepskin jersey wrapped around his little legs and her kappie on his head.

The bitter cold wind blew a little softer that day, over the frozen fields of the eastern Free State.

The *Homeward Bound*

In July 1883 more settlers arrived at the Marburg Mission Station run by the Reverend Stoppel, on the Natal South Coast near Port Shepstone. By September 1883 there were 246 Norwegians, 175 Britons and 112 Germans all settled in the district, having taken up farming or trading in the surrounding district.

Unfortunately, there was a terrible depression in Natal during the 1880s and this affected the area very badly, so much so, in fact, that even the local shipping service that had sprung up was curtailed. As a result, many of the settlers were driven away from the area in search of work.

Three of these unfortunate Norwegian settlers were Inguald and Bernhard Nilsen and Zefanias Oslen. They wandered up the coast, finding part-time work to keep body and soul together, and at Durban they decided to turn inland towards the Drakensburg in search of work on the farms that were now being populated by the incoming farmers. They eventually reached the Witzieshoek area of the Free State, and there, in that most beautiful part of the country, they found employment on one of the local farms.

With the passage of time, however, they all became extremely homesick, and longed to visit their families and relatives. Being seafaring men they decided to build a seaworthy boat and designed a four-and-three-quarter ton vessel with an overall length of 6 m, a beam of just over 2 m and drawing 1,3 m of water. After buying the necessary materials they started construction. As they could only work on the boat in their

14

spare time, the task was long and arduous and she took about eighteen months to complete. They christened her *Homeward Bound* and she was ready for her laborious journey down to Durban in February 1886.

They lashed her to a long-wheelbase transport wagon, inspanned a team of oxen and proceeded to the coast. Towards the end of March that year they arrived in Durban. The people of the town could not believe it. This was certainly the first sea-going vessel ever to come from the Free State and when the townsfolk heard that they planned to sail back to Norway, they were aghast. After many parties and much pomp and ceremony on 2 May 1886 they raised the sails on the *Homeward Bound* and put to sea. The newspapers were full of the story, the international press was informed, and her passage was watched with intense interest and concern by the world. Her every known movement was charted and passing ships instructed to report on her progress. The voyage was extremely hazardous as, being such a small craft, she had to hug the coastline. Whenever stormy weather threatened she would have to heave to, in a suitably protected bay along the coast, wait out the weather and then set forth once more. Everywhere they docked along the way they were met by tumultuous welcomes and fanfare, and treated as celebrities.

On 20 March 1887, a full ten months after setting sail from Durban, this tiny craft sailed into Dover harbour, to the twin sprays of salute from the harbour tug, every ship's foghorn blaring a welcome and a full military band playing. The crowd of people lining the pier went mad with excitement.

They were feted and feasted by royalty and London society. So famous had their incredible feat become that Queen Victoria ordered that the little boat be hoisted out of the water and put on public exhibition at the Crystal Palace. The sale of the *Homeward Bound,* plus a generous public grant, ensured its brave crew a luxurious trip back to their motherland from England, after which these three brave Norwegians, all the way from Witzieshoek in the Free State, disappeared from the pages of the world press, never to be heard of again.

The Natal Native Contingent

It was January 1879 in Natal, Sir Bartle Frere's ultimatum had expired and Britain was at war with the Zulu people. But the senior officers soon realised that they did not have sufficient troops at their disposal and it was decided to raise a corps of irregular horse troops from among the local black people to offset the shortage of regulars. This 'Natal Native Contingent' (NNC) comprised volunteers from tribes that had fled south of the Tugela from Shaka. The Hlubi, Amangwani and Mangwe all had scores to settle with the Zulu. This story revolves around the 'Edendale Contingent' a troop of deeply religious men from the settlement of Edendale just outside Pietermaritzburg.

Edendale was one of the finest Christian mission settlements ever. The land was owned by the inhabitants, bought and paid for by themselves. A strongly Wesleyan community possessing schools and a church, this settlement was led by three fathers, all of them preachers and class leaders.

One of the three, Daniel M'Simang, upon receiving the message from the Government calling for volunteers, said: 'We have sat in the shadow of the Great White Queen in security and peace for many years, we have enjoyed privileges and grown well, our children have a good education. Shall we not obey her when she calls for the services of her dark children...?' The response was immediate – 'We will!'

The fathers of the settlement undertook to bear the expenses of that voluntary troop. They provided the horses, the saddles and all the stores.

The British Army gave them very little and treated them rather contemptuously. All the young men of the settlement volunteered their services and it fell to the elders to choose the best hundred men. And very well they did their job. These were the finest, proudest black soldiers ever seen. Many of the volunteers were married with children.

On the day of their departure, a solemn service was held to commend the men to the care of the Almighty. Then quiet farewells were exchanged between mothers and sons, husbands and wives, and the troop began to march away. A little way out of the settlement, the elders stopped and led the men in prayer and then handed over to Sergeant Major Simeon Kambule, one of the settlement leaders. The old men returned to Edendale to pray.

When the volunteers joined the regular forces of the British Army, they were given only mealies and rough beef as rations. Simeon Kambule made representation to the officers and requested normal rations, including bread, tea, sugar and coffee. This was refused. Simeon quietly informed the officers that they would provide rations at their own expense and that they would serve without Government rations until some officer could decide upon their status.

I don't want to go into the battle of Isandlwana here. Suffice it to say that Simeon Kambule managed to extricate his few remaining men from that disastrous battle, forded the Mzinyathi River at Fugitives Drift and rode for Helpmekaar.

In Pietermaritzburg two irregular troopers arrived exhausted and desperate for food and water. They blurted out the terrible news and were promptly thrown into jail, lest they cause panic by spreading the news. Another two arrived and told the Edendale Elders of the disaster and David M'Simang said, 'If this be true, the Great White Queen will need every one of her children to fight for this country. We will go and raise another troop from Edendale.' Once more, fully equipped by the fathers, another Edendale troop was raised and hastened to the front.

Natal now lay at the mercy of the Zulus, and it was only because of the strict orders of King Cetshwayo that the colony was not invaded. The losses were appalling and troops so scarce that the dead lay for four months on the battlefield of Islandlwana until reinforcements arrived. The enlarged Edendale troop guarded the colony's borders and helped to prepare for the next advance to Ulundi, the capital of Zululand. Since their great deeds at Isandlwana, their worth had been realised and they now, for the first time, received normal rations as well as pay from the British Army.

The contingent fought in every single battle, acquitting themselves excellently and winning the admiration of every British officer who came into contact with them. Every morning they would rise one hour prior to their schedule in order to hold family prayers. Every man was present and every evening, no matter what time, they would all gather for the evening service.

On the morning of the Battle of Ulundi, the final battle of the Anglo-Zulu War, Captain Shepstone, their commanding officer, was lying asleep when he heard the sound of singing. He recognised the hymn and sheepishly arose and joined his troops in worship, knowing full well that many of them would not return that night.

The battle that day was terrible and when the Zulus were put to flight, the Edendale Contingent was among those ordered to pursue them – and they were the last to return to the camp that night. Shepstone, utterly exhausted, threw himself down on a blanket, glad to be alive. He heard the sound of singing. His men were singing a Methodist hymn before even seeking food or rest. 'God forgive me', he said, 'they are thanking the Lord for their lives', and he joined his men in worship.

When the war was over, Simeon Kambule was awarded the Distinguished Service Medal. I believe that had he been white he would have received the Victoria Cross. The British did not give the Natal Native Contingent the praise and the glory that it rightly deserved. No wonder the people of Edendale lost respect for white people, and it does not surprise me that, during the apartheid era, there was so much trouble in that area.

The SS *Mendi*

It is my belief that our written history has done a grave injustice to Shaka and the Zulu people. We have received a jingoed and biased version of that particular era, fed to us by the likes of Fynn and Owen, etc. who had agendas of their own. The discipline, the sense of self-worth and courage instilled in that people was still evident nearly a century after the death of their great warrior-king. On the night of 20 February 1917 the commandeered liner SS *Mendi* was carrying hundreds of black South African troops, the majority of them Zulus, across the English Channel, bound for Le Havre and then on to the front line in Flanders. Under wartime regulations, she was ploughing through the Channel with no lights when another darkened vessel crashed into her and she began to sink rapidly. Every man as he came up from below, went straight to his appointed place, stood to attention, and awaited further instructions. The scene that followed was one of the most extraordinary and heroic of that terrible war.

A Zulu clergyman addressed the men: 'Be quiet and calm my Countrymen, for what is taking place is exactly what you came to do – you are going to die... Brothers, we will drill the Death Drill. I, a Zulu, say that you are my brothers. Swazi, Pondo, Sotho. We die like brothers. Let me hear your war cries!'

On the tilting, darkened deck those black soldiers stripped. Barefoot and naked, the way their ancestors went into battle, against the noise of the wind, crashing seas and creaking plates of the doomed vessel, they began stamping their bare feet in the death drill, celebrating their onrushing death with the war songs that Shaka had taught them. It was a scene, the survivors declared, that would be burnt into their memories forever – those singing men slipping into their cold grave in the English Channel.

Back in South Africa, the Prime Minister, the renowned Boer War General Louis Botha, moved a motion of sympathy for the bereaved families and friends and, spontaneously, the entire white Parliament rose to their feet and bowed their heads in respect for those brave warriors, the only occasion on which such a tribute to black example was ever paid.

I believe the time has come to rewrite our magnificent history. This time much more objectively and to recognise blacks as truly worthy in their own right.

Women's roles in Pilgrim's Rest

F ist-fighting and wrestling matches there were in plenty, and a great deal of drunkenness. But no reports of murders or serious assaults. There was none of the brandishing of pistols and exchanges of shots at short range that made the gold diggers in other parts of the world notorious.

The diggers had a sense of comradeship. They were not very free with information when it came to pegging claims, for then it was 'every man for himself', but they helped one another and were generous when a man was down on his luck. There was one ghastly exception to this rule and the story is still being told over a hundred years later.

An Englishman named George Grey and his partner set out one day in 1873 to walk the 240 km to Delagoa Bay, where they were to buy supplies and then tramp back to the diggings. Somewhere in the foothills of the Lebombo Mountains, Grey developed malaria and became so ill that he could not walk any further. His companion made camp, put food and water and a loaded rifle beside the sick man and then made a dash for Delagoa Bay, intending to return with more food and medicine.

He arrived at the little Portuguese settlement and went into a canteen for a drink … and another … and another. He was drunk for ten days. When at last he sobered up and walked back to camp, Grey was dead and hyenas surrounded the remains of his body.

The scandal of the day was the importation of African women from the Portuguese territory. Before the wagon road to Delagoa Bay, supplies were carried to the diggings by porters. Among them would be a bevy of buxom girls who thought nothing of walking 300 km through the bush (today the Kruger National Park) with cases of 'squareface' gin, on their heads. The Portuguese who ran these caravans were not content with selling the gin. They sold the girls too. Many of them never returned to their own country, but settled down as 'housekeepers'.

The Reverend Gerald Herring, in his history of Pilgrim's Rest, describes a Christmas Eve outside one of the pubs:

> … [A] number of men came into camp to celebrate the festive season. A number of their dusky ladies had the temerity to wander in too, but for this freedom they had to pay. A large barrel stood in the middle of the street. It was half full of water. Into it the men dropped coins for which the women struggled. The awkward and inelegant posture taken up by necessity by each competitor in turn furnished the diggers with their opportunity. The valley echoed with laughter and the smack-smack of hard and heavy hands.

It was obviously time for the first white women to appear upon the scene, to turn the shacks and tents into homes and reshape the manners and morals of the community. The first woman there was Mrs Tom McLachlan who lived in a stone house at Mac-Mac. She was there in 1872 and helped many a fever-stricken traveller who had crossed the Lowveld from Delagoa Bay, only to collapse on the track that led up the mountainside to the diggings.

Mrs Dietricks, wife of a German officer, arrived with her husband in 1873. Dietricks was the assistant to MacDonald, Mining Commissioner of the district. They had two daughters, one of whom became Mrs Elsa Smithers, who set down her recollections of Pilgrim's Rest in a book called *March Hare*.

Elsa recounted the story of Miss Elizabeth Russel who lived in a tent on the diggings and worked on a claim of her own, often standing knee-deep in water. There were two Russel girls – Elizabeth, who was called Bessie, and Annie. They were the daughters of Mr H B Russel, a well-known citizen of Heidelberg and Pretoria, in both of which towns he established himself in business as a miller and merchant during the 1870s.

Mr Russel forbade his daughters to go to the diggings, but Elizabeth defied him and she and her brother Alfred, better known as 'Tucker' Russel, made their way there and acquired a claim in the creek. Their father was extremely angry when he found out that he had been disobeyed, and the rest of the family was forbidden to communicate with the runaways. The two were warned that if they could not pay their way, they should not expect help from the family. Mr Russel must have forgiven them at some stage, however, for Elizabeth was later married from the family home in Pretoria.

She certainly earned her place in the history of the Transvaal, for she not only went to the diggings, and worked a claim there at a time when such conduct by a young woman was regarded as scandalous, but she made a success of the venture. As a schoolteacher her salary had been £25 per annum. One of her claims at Pilgrim's Rest is reputed to have earned her a profit of £200 per month for some considerable time.

All in all, Elizabeth seems to have been a young woman well ahead of her time. She had been born in London on 29 May 1850 and came to South Africa with her parents in 1855. They settled in Pietermaritzburg, Natal, where Mr Russel ran the Boston Mills and the girls were sent to Cheltenham House School in Pinetown. She left school at the age of sixteen to become a governess and later taught at Caversham in Natal. Her father and the rest of the family settled at Heidelberg in the Transvaal, where Mr Russel opened a store. Elizabeth went to Harrismith where she ran a private school of sorts and took in music pupils as well. She worked her income up to about £25 per month and managed to buy a piano for £75. Then came the news of the discovery of gold in the Lydenburg district. She and her brother Tucker decided to try their luck at the diggings. She sold her piano, bought thirty bags of wheat, picks and shovels, blankets and food. She also made a tent of heavy canvas. At last the two of them set out, with the reproaches and warnings of their parents still ringing in their ears.

Elizabeth had shown sound business acumen in taking with her a cargo of wheat. She had it milled on the way down to Lydenburg and sold the flour at a very handsome profit.

The young Russels found to their surprise quite a number of their Natal acquaintances in Pilgrim's Rest. They pitched their tent near that of Captain Dietricks and his wife, who were old friends of the Russels. Elizabeth was fortunate in finding that Yankee Dan, one of the best known of the old diggers, was prepared to act as her advisor and he guided her around many a pitfall.

She and her brother had no luck with the first claim, so they decided to move to the middle of the camp, where she pegged another claim. They were employing eight local men to do the hard labour and their funds were beginning to run out, so Elizabeth set up another business on the sideline, the manufacture of sausage rolls and ginger beer, which sold remarkably well. While she was busy with this, young Tucker started slacking. This precipitated a family row and Tucker left in a huff.

Elizabeth then moved her tent to the middle camp and fired all her staff except one man, nicknamed 'Basket', whom she set to work under her supervision. One day, after much fruitless digging, he rushed into her tent doing a war dance and handed her a nugget weighing four ounces. Basket had saved the day! The claim was a rich one and Elizabeth, joined by her other brother Harry, began to make substantial profits.

Working a claim near them at that time was a young American named William A B Cameron. Elizabeth liked his enterprising spirit and his looks and they were soon engaged. President Burgers attended the wedding and the local paper, *Die Volkstem,* described it as a golden wedding, a subtle reference to the fact that both the bride and groom were gold miners. The paper's reporter referred to Miss Russel as 'the young lady genius of the diggings'. The President proposed the toast to the bride and groom.

Soon after this, Cameron was elected to represent the Lydenburg diggers in the Volksraad. In 1876, he and his wife went to the United States to attend, as official representatives of the Zuid-Afrikaansche Republiek, an international exhibition being held in Philadelphia.

After their return to South Africa, Elizabeth and her husband found that they were incompatible and separated, never to meet again. She was left with five children and her struggle to feed, clothe and educate them would make a story in its own right. This fearless, forthright woman, one of the true pioneers of our beautiful land, to whom Pilgrim's Rest must raise a monument one day, was eighty years of age when she died in Volksrust in May 1931.

Thomas Burgers

W hen Martinus Wessels Pretorius resigned as President of the Transvaal Republic, many Volksraad members were in favour of President Brand of the Orange Free State taking office in order to promote closer unity between the two Republics. But he wisely refused and recommended Thomas Francois Burgers.

Thomas Burgers was thirty-seven, fond of music, well educated, with liberal and progressive views acquired through study and extensive travel, and happily married to a Scots lass, Mary Bryson. His only blemish was that he had fallen out with his church by saying that the Devil had no tail, but he eventually won the argument in the Cape Supreme Court and was reinstated by the Synod.

On 1 July 1872 he was sworn in as President. He inherited a bankrupt Republic and the first of his many heroic actions was to borrow £60 000 from a Cape bank, guarantee it personally, buy up the worthless blue-back banknotes and stave off the financial crisis. But alas, this was to be one of the many instances that proved to him the truth of the old proverb that 'the road to hell is paved with good intentions'.

He had passed the Education Act instituting an extensive Government Education system, the first ever in the Transvaal, introducing also non-doctrinal religious teaching. The Boers, most of them staunch Calvinists, called these Godless schools! Many conservative Boers did not like the fact that he had married an English-speaking woman and when he eventually moved a piano into his house, this was felt to be the last straw.

Singing was done only on Sundays in Church. Poor Thomas Burgers enlightened visionary – that insidious political poison took its toll.

He went abroad and negotiated a loan to build the railway line from Pretoria to Delagoa Bay, but upon his return, found the Transvaal in a complete mess. The Mac Mac Goldfields had been discovered in 1873 and the miners wanted roads and provisions. The Doppers said that the train was the anti-Christ. The Venda were attacking the still lawless Soutpansberg area and the Pedi were killing and plundering in the Lydenburg district. Very few men volunteered for commando duties and Paul Kruger, who had disliked Burgers from the outset, refused to lead the commando. So Burgers did it himself and with the help of some 2 500 Swazi volunteers, was successful until the commando got 'huis toe' disease and melted away.

Burgers decided to build two forts in the Lydenburg district and to raise a mercenary army. He appointed Conrad Hans von Schlickman as Commandant to head up the Lydenburg Volunteers at Fort Burgers and Ignatius Ferreira of the Middleburg Volunteers to garrison Fort Weeber. Unfortunately for Burgers, the English were watching all this from Natal and on 12 April 1877 Sir Theophilus Shepstone rode into Pretoria to annex the Transvaal in the name of Queen Victoria and none other than the author, Rider Haggard, raised the Union Jack.

Thomas Burgers died in the Cape Province in 1881, embittered, broken and impoverished. One of his last requests was that he be buried at the entrance to the sheep kraal so that the hoofs of the animals would obliterate the grave of a man who had failed. He was a decent, conscientious man who had tried desperately to save the Boers from their own folly and in-fighting, which inevitably lost them their country, and set the stage for two tragic wars that embittered the politics of the country for a century afterwards.

In 1895 his body was disinterred and with due honour taken to Pretoria where he now rests in peace.

The story of Dina Chambers

The old, now deserted town of Schoemansdal was certainly once a
busy town with a vigorous crowd of inhabitants and plenty of
interest and excitement. Inevitably, there were many quarrels and
fights. The truculent Commandant-General Schoeman was the centre of
most of the local upheavals, and one of these quarrels started an epic
venture both fantastic and heroic.

When quarrels culminated in the unhappy Burgher Civil War in
Pretoria, Schoeman gathered his supporters in the town named after him.
He decided to seize the town's defensive armament, which comprised
two muzzle-loading cannons of the type known as 'Ou Grietjie'.

This act enraged the burghers of Schoemansdal, for it left the town
defenceless against the local Africans, who were in a very belligerent
mood on account of the occupation of their land by the Boers. Hard
words were freely bandied about. Piet Eloff, the Veldkornet, and John
Chambers, a deserter from the British army who had settled in the town
in 1849 and married a local twenty-year old Afrikaner maiden, Dina
Gertruida Fourie, were particularly articulate. The bitter wrangling
eventually led to Chambers' swearing that he would blow Schoeman to
the Devil before he would let him take the guns away from the town.

Schoeman finally galloped off on his horse, threatening Chambers
with dire retribution when times were more opportune. Periodically
threats and abuse reached Chambers from Pretoria, as a reminder that
Schoeman had not forgotten. When a rumour reached Chambers in 1858

that Schoeman had actually set out on his vengeful return, he decided to leave the town for the safety of the wilderness.

So, on 5 June 1859 John Chambers, his wife Dina and their four children, with one of Dina's brothers, David Fourie, who was a keen hunter, and one Jakobus Lottering and his wife and child, left Schoemansdal and headed for the eastern bushveld. Along the banks of the Luvuvhu River, sometimes known as the Phaphuli (Pafuri), from the Venda clan of that name, they followed in the tracks of the unfortunate Van Rensburg trek. As they travelled, hunting and prospecting, malevolent mosquitoes started to take their toll, and one by one the party sickened. But they pressed on.

First Lottering's wife died and was buried in a now long-forgotten grave. Then the child followed her mother and soon the Chambers children also sickened. But on they pressed, shooting elephants and prospecting in the bush. Through the lonely Lebombo range, they reached the flats of Mozambique with its endless miles of heat and bush. The evil tsetse flies were busy at their oxen and at the Save River, all their spans died. Abandoning their wagons, the whole party set off on foot. On the way David Fourie died and Lottering, having lost his entire family, parted company with the Chambers family and wandered off to prospect on his own, returning later to the Transvaal.

The Chambers family trudged on towards Sofala, that dreary little port whose name has always been associated with tales of gold, ivory and the slave trade. They reached Sofala on 8 November 1859, and the hospitable Portuguese did their best to make them comfortable after so cruel a journey.

All four of the Chambers children had died. Wandering through the insalubrious streets of the ancient port of gold, Chambers sickened of Africa and resolved to take his wife and himself off to England. In order to raise funds for this trip, he decided to return to the abandoned wagons and burn them to obtain the iron used in their construction. This he planned to barter with the Africans in exchange for ivory, which he would then sell to finance the passage to England.

Leaving Dina in the care of the Portuguese Governor, Chambers returned safely to the wagons. He burned them and spent a couple of months trading and hunting with a friendly local chief named Sewane.

But by then the busy mosquitoes had worked their insidious poison. Chambers fell sick and, seeing death come stealing out of the bushveld glades to take him, he called for Sewane. 'You and I have been good friends', he said, 'I beg of you a favour. Take the ivory and all my possessions. Exchange them for food and money and take my wife from Sofala back to her parents in the Transvaal.'

So it happened that one morning, there strode into drowsy Sofala the warrior Induna Makakikiyane and fifty stalwart men. They bartered their load of ivory with the Goan merchants and then presented themselves at the Governor's house. 'Your man has sent us to fetch you', they told the excited Dina, and showed her some of his possessions – but not another word would they say.

Gaily she packed her possessions, thanked the anxious Portuguese and the Governor and set off into the wilderness with fifty-one taciturn warriors marching protectively around her. When they were attacked by hostile Africans, she was guarded. When she sickened and wearied, they built a litter and carried her, and fed her on venison and wild fruits.

When finally they reached the old chief's kraal, Dina looked around eagerly for her husband and, silently, Sewane led her to his grave. In grief and loneliness she lay and almost died of misery and fever. For some weeks the inscrutable tribeswomen cared for her, nursing her with herbs of the veld and ancient remedies that only they knew.

Then the Induna came with his fifty warriors and the litter. They had promised her husband to take her home and this they would, be she dead or alive. They picked her up and set off through the bush, having at times to fight off hostile tribes and robbers, as well as wild animals. So precarious was the journey that they could not even light a fire at night, for fear of attracting the attention of the marauding bands that infested the countryside at that time.

Sometimes Dina walked and sometimes she was carried. The Save River was full when they reached it, so the warriors made a raft. For a whole day they laboured to cross the mighty river, while its chocolate-coloured floodwaters surged down past them, laden with driftwood and floating islands of vegetation. Beyond the river they trudged on. One morning, as they were travelling through a forest of baobab trees, one of the warriors suddenly called Dina and led her to a tree. Beneath it was a mound of stones, and on the trunk was carved a name. It was Dina's father. He had heard, through the mysterious, apparently telepathic, system by which news travels through the African bush, that the Chambers' party was in trouble. The old man, together with his son Gert, had set out to rescue them. Then the mosquitoes had come and there, beneath the baobab tree, he slept forever.

This fresh blow prostrated Dina. She lay and wept in her misery, and would have willingly abandoned herself to death. Around her, the puzzled warriors stood and wondered what had caused her grief, for, as they had no language in common, the carving on the tree was meaningless to them. But the warriors had their orders. They picked her up, bundled her weeping onto the litter and plodded on. Four months and twenty-eight days it took them before they eventually reached the Limpopo River, 320 km from their village. By then Dina was almost dead. On the bank of the river she carved a despairing message onto a piece of wood and sent it off with a runner.

João Albassini, in his fort, received the message and passed it on immediately to Dina's brother Gert. Riding post-haste to the river 120 km away, he met her and carried her back to the kindly care of the Albassini family. It was on the first day of March 1861 that Dina returned to civilisation. The gallant and faithful bodyguards, who had been so true to their promise, tramped down a few days later and were feasted, given presents and thanked. They were then seen off, with much pomp and ceremony, back to the wilds from where they had come.

Dina rested with the Albassini family until she was completely recovered. Then having made her unwilling bow on the stage of history, she returned to the obscure wings again, but not without a final curtain of happiness. While convalescing at the Albassinis she met a certain Jan Hemelyn, whom she married two years later and with whom she lived to a ripe age with some happiness, as compensation for her former pain.

As for Schoemansdal, it marvelled for a while at her poignant adventure and then soon forgot. Its own story was to be tragic enough and, in its own tears, it had little time for sympathy with the troubles of others.

The King of
the Hottentots

In H E Hockley's excellent book on the 1820 Settlers, there is a paragraph recalling that during the reign of James I of England, some men who had been condemned to death for various crimes were given the option of proceeding to the Cape of Good Hope (Saldania, as it was then known), to start a settlement there. The leader of this band, elected by his fellow convicts, was a gentleman rogue, one James Crosse, a convicted highwayman who had once been a captain of the Yeomanry. They later established themselves on Robben Island, making periodic sorties to the mainland. Unfortunately, on one of these trips their boat was wrecked on the island, effectively marooning them. This amazing story of who the first white settlers at the Cape really were was uncovered by John Cope of South Africa and researched mostly in Britain.

However, to digress slightly, some time before this, in May 1613, a British East Indiaman, the *Hector,* was anchored in Table Bay. The chief of the local Khoikhoi, named Xhoré, was lured aboard together with one of his men and taken back to England. His companion died on the voyage, but Xhoré was made of sterner stuff. In London he stayed with Sir Thomas Smythe and was taught the English language and observed English customs and way of life. Xhoré stayed in London for almost a year, and was then put aboard the *Hector.* On 18 June 1614, he set foot back on Cape soil, wearing a new suit of brass armour that had been specially made for him.

To return to the story of the English convicts at the Cape. The Newgate

Prison records tell us that there were a total of seventeen condemned men given the option of either being hanged or banished to the Cape. One escaped in the ship's pinnace after sailing from Sandwich, two were taken on to India, and four died of scurvy during the passage.

The ten remaining men were set ashore at the Cape with provisions, weapons (but no guns) and a long boat in case of trouble. When the fleet departed, the local Khoikhoi became hostile as Xhoré had related his London experiences and said that the whites were going to take over the Khoikhoi land and there was nothing anybody could do to stop them. How very prophetic his words were to prove! He had witnessed the awesome might of the British army, and he suggested that they get rid of these people post-haste. Four of the unsuspecting men set out to visit Xhoré's village and were ambushed along the way. One was killed outright and two others wounded. They made it back to camp and, along with the others, fled to Robben Island in the longboat, which as related above was later wrecked.

Eventually, a passing vessel, the *New Year Gift,* commanded by Captain Martin Pring, sailed into Table Bay on 1 March 1616. Xhoré came down to the beach and told the sailors that Captain Crosse and his men were living on the island. Pring immediately sent over the ship's pinnace, which returned with three of the Newgate men. Captain Pring's log tells us how Captain Crosse, seeing the ship at anchor, made a raft out of the now wrecked longboat and, together with two other men, tried to row out to the vessel. The raft capsized, however, and they drowned. The *Gift* then set sail for England with the three men who were willing to go back to England.

The remaining three men decided not to risk going back. Perhaps they were right, because the *Gift* had been anchored at Sandwich for no more than two hours when the three escaped overboard. Being penniless and hungry, they stole a purse from an old woman in the town and the constabulary found them in the local tavern, drinking ale. When the records were checked, they realized that these men had been condemned to death. They were taken to Hanging Fields just outside of Sandwich and suitably dispatched.

The fate of the three who stayed behind is a mystery, for when another fleet arrived with more convicts three months later, there was no sign of them. The convicts on this fleet begged to be hanged in preference to being left there, but in vain. Commodore Joseph's orders were clear, so he sailed away without them. Luckily for them however, the *Swan* came to their aid. Captain Davis took pity on them and transported them to India. Thus it was in 1616, a full thirty-six years before the coming of Jan van Riebeeck, that the first white settlers at the Cape came to a sticky end. The English abandoned the Cape, and it cost them three expensive expeditions and two battles before they got it back again in 1806.

Alfred Aylward, the Lydenburg Volunteers and the Gunn of Gunn

During the latter half of his incumbency, the unfortunate Thomas Burgers, President of the Transvaal Republic, raised two mercenary forces. The Middelburg Volunteers were placed at Fort Weeber under Commandant Ignatius Ferreira. Conrad Hans von Schlickman, an experienced Captain who had served in the Prussian Army during the Franco-Prussian War, was placed in charge of the Lydenburg Volunteers at Fort Burgers. Burgers appointed as a recruiting agent in Kimberley, an unusual character named Alfred Aylward who, after a dubious period in journalism, instigated the miners to rise in the so-called Black Flag Rebellion in Kimberley. The High Commissioner's response was to send the 24th Regiment of Foot marching up to Kimberley, all the way from Cape Town, a distance of some 960 km. Aylward got wind of the Regiment's approach and the Black Flag Rebellion petered out. In October of 1876 Aylward, with seventy 'rough diamonds' recruited from the bars and the ranks of the unemployed, was already making his way northward towards Fort Burgers.

A short digression may be in order here to trace the subsequent fortunes of the 24th Regiment of Foot. They were turned around at Kimberley and marched all the way to Grahamstown, a distance of some 750 km, where they took part in the Ninth Frontier War. When the war was over they were marched to Durban, re-kitted and marched to Isandlwana where they died almost to a man. To hear that story told most superbly you must hear it from David Rattray of Fugitives Drift.

But to return to the main story. In September of 1876 Mpehle led an attack on Fort Burgers and, sweeping down from the heights of Marone, captured forty-three head of cattle. The Volunteers who had given chase were ambushed in a ravine and spears rained down on them from the heights. Lieutenant Krapp and George Robus died in the skirmish. The arrival of Aylward and his motley international crew was most welcome. Von Schlickman led his force northwards in a raid against the Pedi. Their plan was to raid some kraals in a valley some 15 km away, known as Mehera's Kloof, but the Pedi guide led them into a well-laid ambush. The kraals were found abandoned and when the Volunteers entered a narrow valley, the Pedi opened fire on them. In the fight, Von Schlickman was mortally wounded and the dead and the dying were carried back on crude litters made of torn shirts and handkerchiefs. The entire episode had been a disaster. Aylward had to wait until December for his formal appointment as Commandant following the death of Von Schlickman. But his greatest rival was yet to come.

On 20 December 1876 there arrived in Pretoria one of the most astonishing personalities ever to strut the stage of Transvaal history. His name was Charles Grant Murray Somerset Stuart Gunn, a highland laird with the title of 'The Gunn of Gunn and the Lord of Farquhar'. A handsome man some thirty-six years of age, he claimed that he had served in the 13th Hussars from the age of sixteen and had fled to South Africa in 1871 after killing a man in a duel. He arrived in Pretoria accompanied by twenty-two recruits for the Lydenburg Volunteers, all dressed in blue Hussar tunics with yellow braid, white caps, colourless cord riding-breeches and stockings. This assembly of men he drilled up and down Market Square in full view of the Volksraad and President Burgers. The Gunn had a very glib tongue. He dropped names of British aristocrats and spoke airily of having been awarded both the Victoria and the Iron Cross in sundry hair-raising adventures. In constant attendance upon his person were two lackeys and a highland piper. Night after night, The Gunn entertained guests at the Pretoria Hotel whilst the piper made the night hideous by striding up and down, squeezing out paeans of praise to his lord and master. Everybody from the President down was extremely impressed with Gunn's outfit and the Transvaal Government immediately hired them, dispatching them to the frontier to join forces with Aylward.

After recruiting nine more men in Pretoria, the Laird and his self-styled 'Gunn Highlanders' left for the 'Front'. The journey to Lydenburg was marked by their excesses. They drank, made free with the farmers' fruit and poultry, hogs and daughters, and generally had the surrounding countryside by the ear. At Lydenburg The Gunn, in no hurry to get to Fort Burgers, lingered for some time. He loved to 'do the polite' to the ladies and on such occasions his kilted piper, dressed in full regalia, would precede his master and parade up and down outside making music. Stafford Parker, the former President of the Diamond Diggers Republic, had settled in Lydenburg and The Gunn had selected Parker's wife for one of these visits. Everything went according to plan except that the passage outside the drawing room ended in a dark corner and a steep flight of stairs. The dark corner proved the end of the piper as well. Carried away by his music, he tumbled down the stairs, sending the screams of a million Scottish demons from his pipes as his head went through the bag, ending his music for quite some time.

The end of The Gunn of Gunn was not so sudden. After spending Christmas in Lydenburg, he marched his 'Gunn Highlanders' up to Fort Burgers, claiming that President Burgers himself had appointed him to take command of the fort. Aylward, however, was well prepared, having been expecting this sort of thing for quite some time now. The news of The Gunn's activities had preceded him by weeks. A number of the Highlanders had already been arrested at Krugerspost for riotous behaviour and when The Gunn arrived at Fort Burgers, he found he had met his match.

His men were drawn up on the parade ground and Alfred Aylward promptly ran out a cannon on their flank, ordering them, one and all, to lay down their arms. Nonplussed, the Highlanders obeyed. Aylward then gave them a dressing down, but not too harshly, as his adjutant reminded him that he himself had been a rebel of some renown.

The Gunn and a few of his cronies were immediately arrested, while the other men were accepted into the corps. The Gunn was sent back to Pretoria to stand trial on various charges of public disturbance, found guilty and sent to gaol. When Theophilus Shepstone raised the British flag in Pretoria in April 1877 and annexed the Transvaal for the Crown, one of his first acts was to declare a general amnesty for prisoners and fugitives from justice in the Transvaal. And of course, one of those to walk out of gaol was The Gunn of Gunn. But such characters hardly ever learn their lesson and, after a scandal caused by his alleged liaison with the wife of Colonel Weatherley, The Gunn melts away into the shadows of history, never to be heard of again.

Scotty Smith

If ever there was a character in our history who, along with Dick Turpin, Ned Kelly and Jesse James, deserves a place in the rogue's gallery of the world's 'Gentlemen of the Road', it is our very own Scotty Smith. He is notorious as a cattle rustler, horse thief, highwayman and outlaw, secret service agent, IDB trafficker, confidence trickster, soldier of fortune and half a dozen other things besides. He was loved, feared and hated throughout the northern borders of South Africa for almost three decades and, as a young boy, I knew of the Welcome Beer Hall in Potchefstroom, where the bullet holes in the counter were a reminder of one of his escapades.

Born George St Leger Gordon Lennox in 1845, the eldest son of a Perthshire landowner, he received a good education, which included subjects such as land surveying and veterinary science. He landed in Cape Town in 1877 and for the next forty years this country was his home and was where he earned his dubious fame.

At the end of 1877 Scotty was in Kokstad, working as a military farrier, when he received a message that his bank in Glasgow required his presence. He calmly deserted his regiment, went to Scotland, sorted things out and returned, only to be punished for dereliction of duty. He was sent to King William's Town, where he decided that army life was not for him, and so began his long career in brigandage. His desertion set the pattern for the future. He commandeered two of the best police horses, and scarpered!

It is totally impossible to recount the events of this man's doings in any coherent order, so I am going to set down some of the better known escapades of this fascinating man.

This story is probably the first of his escapades as it took place shortly after his desertion from the army. In his old age, he was extremely proud of this particular event and understandably so, because in subsequent exploits he never quite reached the same heights of ingenuity.

He rode from King William's Town to Fort Beaufort, where he sold the two stolen horses and, with his real identity undetected, he took on a job as an assistant foreman with a road construction gang. He and the foreman soon became good friends and, as the road under construction passed through many farms, they were entertained hospitably by many farmers, including one particular elderly couple, at whose home there was always a bed and a hot meal awaiting them.

Unfortunately, the old man died and, at the reading of the will, an amazing disclosure was made. Practically all he possessed had been bequeathed to the lawyer, while his wife was left penniless. Hurriedly, the lawyer wound up the estate and placed the assets up for auction. Almost £10 000 was realised and deposited in the lawyer's bank account. The widow, meanwhile, was too frail and heartbroken to challenge the will.

Scotty was not prepared to let this matter rest and, on obtaining a copy of the will, concluded that it was a forgery. He sent it with a covering letter to the bank manager, suggesting that the signature be verified by a handwriting expert. He also decided to take independent action to assist the widow, just in case nothing came of his letter.

On the night on which the money was deposited in the Bank, Scotty was in town and the following morning Fort Beaufort awoke to the electrifying news that the Bank had been robbed of £10 000, with no clues left as to the identity of the thief. A reward of £1 000 was offered for the capture of the thief.

Some time later, Scotty and his foreman were sitting in their camp. The latter looked very worried. 'What's the matter?' asked Scotty.

'It's my wife, she is seriously ill and requires specialist treatment and

40

I haven't the money. But if only I could capture that Bank robber...'

'I think we can rectify that situation', said Scotty. 'First let's get the reward money straightened out.' They set off to the bank.

'I have certain information that could lead to the successful capture of the thief and the return of the money', said Scotty, 'but first we want a written undertaking that the £1 000 reward money will be paid.'

The delighted bank manager drew up the document and signed it. Back at camp, Scotty gave his friend the copy of agreement saying that the money was as good as in his pocket, and informed his friend that he had robbed the bank, and that he should call the police and have him arrested.

'Rubbish', said his friend, 'and even if you had, I would never turn you in.'

Scotty, assured him that no gaol could hold him and promised him that he would remain behind bars only until the reward was paid out. In this way he persuaded his friend to turn him in. Scotty was sent to prison for robbery. The manager, however, would not hand over the reward because after searching Scotty's lodgings, no money could be found. He visited Scotty in gaol and broached the subject of the missing money.

'What have you done about the will?' asked Scotty.

'You were right', was the reply. 'The will was forged and the matter is now in the hands of the police. You did a good thing there, Scotty, the money really does belong to her, which makes it more incomprehensible as to why you stole it.'

'It should be obvious', said Scotty. 'I have no faith in the law, and I was making sure that she received her just due, whatever happened.'

Thereupon, they came to an agreement. Scotty, handcuffed, would show the bank manager where the money was hidden and the widow in turn would receive the money. Scotty led the manager to a mound of earth some distance out of town, slipped his handcuffs, overpowered the manager and tied him up seated on top of the mound. Climbing on to the manager's horse, he said, 'I have never broken my word, and I don't intend to start now. You are sitting on top of the money and I will tell the first person I see in town of your whereabouts and you will be rescued.'

He was true to his word, the bank manager was found and the money recovered. As Scotty had been arrested, the bank paid the reward money to the foreman whose wife could then have the treatment needed, and the widow received her inheritance.

There was a countrywide hue and cry about the audacious gaol breaker, but Scotty was already riding hard for the north-west.

In order to appreciate fully the antics of George St Leger Lennox, it is necessary to have a broad understanding of not only the territory but also the people, places, politics and events of the last quarter of the 19th century. The area we are talking about stretches from Kimberley, westward towards Klaarwater (now Griquatown), then north to Postmasburg and Kuruman, turning east to Mmabatho and Zeerust, south to Mamusa (the present-day Schweizer-Reneke), down to Bloemhof and then back to Kimberley. This is the area that later briefly would be known as the Republics of Goshen and Stellaland.

Various tribes, all engaged in internecine warfare – wonderful pickings for freebooters and filibusters – occupied this area. In the northern part were the two Baralong rivals for power, the pro-British Montsioa at Sehuba and the pro-Boer Moshette at Kunana. In the south were their counterparts, the Batlaping Chief Mankaroane at Taung and the Koranna Chief Massouw at Mamusa. It was a troublemaker's paradise. These various chiefs would hire the freebooters on the usual conditions – retention of half of the booty and half of the farmland taken from the chief's rivals.

But these mercenaries had drawn up a gentleman's agreement amongst themselves, that if they faced each other in battle, they would deliberately aim high. This was so strictly observed, apparently, that only two white men were actually killed in these skirmishes.

The Transvaal freebooters in the north were having a good time. The pro-Boer Chief Moshette had appointed Niklas Gey van Pittius as his agent and with his help, had inflicted a crushing defeat on Montsioa and burnt his capital, Sehuba. The land seized from Montsioa was used for setting up the Boer puppet-republic of Goshen.

In the south, things had gone badly for the pro-British section.

Massouw, the leader of the Koranna, was causing a great deal of trouble. The ancestors of these Koranna had originally lived near Table Bay, but European expansion had forced them ever further to the north-east. Their wanderings had resulted in an almost continuous battle for existence, with all the peoples of the interior viewing them as enemies. They eventually established themselves at Mamusa on the west bank of the Harts River, where they converted a natural hill into a stronghold with a stone fortification on the summit.

In October 1881, Mankaroane and his white mercenaries attacked Mamusa but were defeated by Massouw, who then offered a farm and half the loot captured to every white man who would fight for him. The generous terms attracted a mercenary army of 400 desperadoes under one Sarel Petrus Celliers, who then kept up constant raids on Mankaroane's cattle herds. Poor Mankaroane had fallen out with the English and was also under threat from Gasibone, chief of another rival Batlaping tribe.

To recoup his losses, Mankaroane attacked Massouw at Fourie's Graf, but he suffered a crushing defeat and the very symbol of his power, a ship's cannon, was captured, causing many of his tribesmen to desert him.

This was how matters stood on the wild frontier when Scotty rode into the town of Taung. He was then about thirty-seven, sported a big red beard and had a striking personality. He summed up the situation pretty quickly and offered his assistance to Mankaroane. 'We are too weak to drive the Boers out of our country', Mankaroane told Scotty, 'so we must stop them from settling down, we must raid their camps, we must steal their horses, and keep them shut up in their laager. We must steal their cattle, so that they will be so busy protecting their herds that they won't attack us. When they find that they cannot remain peacefully on the farms, they will get tired and return to their own country.' This I find a very interesting strategy, one not dissimilar from that employed by the Xhosa in the Eastern Cape frontier wars.

Before long Scotty had recruited, organised and armed his own private army consisting of about thirty tough whites and sixty local tribesmen. Scotty and his band threw themselves wholeheartedly into the

43

fray and on more than one occasion, made a clean sweep of the cattle in Boer encampments. He acquired arms and ammunition, clothing and provisions for his men. He had no scruples in breaking into some convenient store. It is known, for example, that he broke into Charles Daly's store in Bloemhof. Daly, incidentally, was himself another interesting character. He had survived the wreck of the *Birkenhead*, was a good friend of Paul Kruger, and was the only man given a magazine licence by the Transvaal Government to supply its forces. However, he arrived one morning to find that the shop had been raided. Pinned to the door was a list of all the stores taken, with a note from Scotty saying that he would pay in due course. The strange thing about this man is that he always kept his word, and there are numerous incidents which proved this.

Scotty's lively band had their own war song, which went like this:

Come saddle up my horse
And strap my billy on
To hell with the Lime Juice Parliament [referring to the Cape]
We'll fight for Mankaroane

Now cheer boys cheer and never be afraid
We're marching in the ranks of the Stellaland Brigade
As we march along, we'll sing this little song
And fight for good old Mankaroane!

There were a few incidents that took place before Scotty formed his little army, and I feel that the following two, in particular, need retelling.

On one occasion, Scotty was in a very tight corner, so hard-pressed by the police in fact that he actually abandoned his horse. By means of some ruse, however, he managed to escape and trekked across the veld on foot. After some time he came across wagon tracks and overtook a few transport riders in charge of three wagons. Scotty asked whose outfit it was. They replied that it was Jan Coetzee's and that he had ridden on ahead as they were so near to home. 'I am Piet Coetzee, Jan Coetzee's nephew', said Scotty. 'You must give me a lift.' He climbed into the wagon, lay down under the tent and went to sleep, to be awoken later by

44

the sound of horses approaching. Somebody asked the transport riders whether they had seen him. When they said they had not, the men turned their horses and rode away in a different direction. On reaching the farm, Scotty brazenly introduced himself to Jan Coetzee as his nephew. In those days most Boer families had so many nephews and nieces that Oom Jan did not doubt Scotty's story at all.

He was immediately invited in, given food and drink and generally made comfortable. All went well until, as was customary, Coetzee and his wife tried to establish to which branch of the family he belonged. Scotty became more and more embarrassed until, cornered, he decided to put his cards on the table. He told them who he was and what had happened and ended up by asking Oom Jan for a horse. 'I haven't any money at the moment, but I promise you faithfully that I will pay you when I can', he said. Oom Jan agreed without question. 'I have heard a great deal about you, Scotty, and how you have helped many people.' True to his word Oom Jan saddled up a good riding chestnut, his wife gave Scotty a satchel of provisions and he rode away. Many months had passed and Oom Jan had forgotten the incident, when Scotty came up to him in Johannesburg Market Square one day and told him he wanted to pay for the horse. Jan Coetzee named a fair price and Scotty promptly paid him double!

Scotty was a master of disguise and this got him out of many tight corners, for example when he was declared the South African Republic's most wanted man, with a price of £500 on his head. Some of the leading Transvaal freebooters, such as Groot Adriaan de la Rey, Niklas Gey van Pittius and Gert van Niekerk were eager to claim the money and they all did their best, but to no avail. On one occasion Groot Adriaan, brother of the famous Boer War General, Koos de la Rey, in a determined effort to capture Scotty, assembled a commando of western Transvaal farmers and set out on his trail. Scotty soon heard about their plan and, instead of doing the sensible thing and going to ground until the danger was over, he decided to play a prank on the posse. After changing the colour of his hair and beard, he set out with a friend and came upon the posse near the village of Amalia. Riding up to the leader he enquired where they were going. 'We are searching for Scotty Smith', came the reply. 'Oh!' Scotty exclaimed, 'my friend and I are also looking for the damned scoundrel! Do you mind if we join you?'

Groot Adriaan agreed to this and so Scotty had the peculiar delight of taking part in a fruitless hunt for himself! This went on for two days. Then Scotty told the Boers that, as he and his friend were now a long way from home, they would have to start back in the morning. He thanked the commando for allowing him to take part in the search and said, 'Every night you have taken it in turn to stand watch, and we've done nothing. As it is our last night, we would like to do our share of guard duty so that you can all have a good night's rest.' The men were only too glad to accept this considerate offer and, needless to say, when they awoke at dawn the next day, not only had Scotty and his friend disappeared, but all the horses had vanished as well.

Though our hero seems to have borne a charmed life, not all freebooters were so lucky. Close to the western border of the Transvaal, not far from Massouw's camp at Manthe, is a deep ravine known as Honey's Kloof. It was here that James Honey, one of the toughest and most reckless of the filibusters, met a sudden and violent death. Honey, a mercenary fighting for the Koranna chief, Massouw, had a bitter quarrel with his fellow adventurers over the distribution of the land and booty. Honey apparently tried to incite the Koranna against them and they decided to have their revenge. They captured him after a struggle and set off back home. It was an extremely hot day when they came upon the spring in the kloof and they went to rest the horses and quench their thirst.

Honey also begged for water. They loosened the riem around his wrists and, as he knelt to drink, one of his captors shot him in the back of the head. Honey toppled slowly over into the stream, staining it red with his blood. The commando then threw his saddle down beside his body and rode away.

African herd boys who found the body reported their find to the authorities and the matter was referred to Sir Charles Warren. As a result Sarel Petrus Celliers, the former commander of Massouw's mercenaries, was arrested along with Gert van Niekerk and others, but owing to lack of evidence, all were later released. However, the story does not end there. According to local legend, shortly after the tragedy, a strange thing happened. To the amazement of the Africans living around Manthe, the eye of the spring began to recede gradually down the kloof until, a year later, it was fully sixty metres away.

The locals swore that Honey's ghost haunted the place and that every year, on the anniversary of the murder, a shot could be plainly heard in the area. 'The spirit that inhabited the spring', they told their children, 'was very angry because the blood of the white man had defiled his waters. So he went to live in another place.'

We leave Scotty himself now and take a brief look at what was happening in that area and how it was affected by larger political events. In July 1882 a peace treaty was drawn up between the Transvaal Government and chief Mankaroane, in terms of which a large portion of Batlaping land was taken away and used to establish the Republic of Stellaland, with Vryburg as its capital. In July 1883, amid great jubilation, the Republic was formally proclaimed by freebooter Gert van Niekerk and its flag – a white star on a green background – was ceremoniously hoisted. Stellaland and Goshen were now nominally independent states, with the Transvaal exercising a vague and ill-defined suzerainty over them.

This was Rhodes' worst nightmare, as the famous Missionary Road seemed likely to be incorporated into the Transvaal and his 'Cape to Cairo' dream was fading fast. So imminent was the danger that Rhodes urged Her Majesty's Government to annex Bechuanaland to forestall the designs of the Germans in South West Africa and the Transvaalers to the east.

The man selected to help maintain peace and order in this unruly area was the Reverend John Mackensie. Mackensie was a zealous political missionary and took very little trouble in hiding his virulently anti-Boer sentiments. The new Commissioner arrived in July 1884 and took strong action immediately. He accepted Montsioa as a British subject, declared the area a British Protectorate, then promptly lowered the one-star flag

47

and raised the Union Jack – all on his own authority. The freebooters went wild. They wanted to lynch him, and there was also huge resentment in the Transvaal Republic. Their Commissioner's action took the British Government completely by surprise and they decided on a complete reversal of policy. They rapped him over the knuckles, ordered the lowering of the British Flag, the raising of the one-star and had him recalled, replacing him with none other than Cecil John Rhodes himself.

Rhodes arrived in Vryheid and, early one morning, went to Niekerksrest on the banks of the Harts River, where he met Van Niekerk, De la Rey and other Stellaland leaders. The Boer mood was very ugly. De la Rey particularly was spoiling for trouble, saying, 'Blood must flow, blood must flow'. But Rhodes knew exactly how to handle this kind of situation. 'Nonsense', he replied. 'I'm hungry. Give me breakfast first, and then we will talk about blood.'

His appeal to traditional Boer hospitality did the trick. Over breakfast the aggression and suspicion gradually subsided and soon they were on friendly terms. Rhodes actually stayed in the Boer camp for a week and became godfather to De la Rey's grandchild. Soon a deal was struck. Rhodes guaranteed the Boers' possession of their farms and cattle and they in turn agreed to accept British rule. Once again the tribes, in this case the Batlaping, lost out on a deal struck between the British and the Boers.

Further north in Goshen, Montsioa was also getting the dirty end of the stick, eventually being forced to surrender practically all of his lands to the freebooters. Gey van Pittius took charge and declared the country Transvaal territory, whilst S J du Toit hoisted the Vierkleur in triumph. On the very same day, Paul Kruger boldly annexed Goshen to the South African Republic. This really put the cat among the pigeons. There was a tremendous outcry at the Cape and Rhodes asked for British military intervention.

Sir Charles Warren set out from the Cape with a large force and arrived in Vryburg early in 1885. Those in favour of British rule were jubilant, but the Transvaal Government's reaction was immediate and dramatic. President Kruger withdrew the annexation proclamation and Du Toit hauled down the Transvaal flag. The southern part of

Bechuanaland, incorporating both Goshen and Stellaland, became a Crown Colony while the northern part became a British Protectorate. The short-lived, inglorious era of the freebooters came to a sudden end.

Meanwhile, Massouw was still causing trouble to the north with his persistent cattle raiding, and the Transvaal government decided to take action. A force of nearly 1 000 men was raised, with the Commandant-General himself, Piet Joubert, in command. Joubert, always a cautious man, upon reaching Mamusa attempted to negotiate a peaceful settlement with the Chief, but the younger members were itching for a fight and, led by one of the more impetuous young Commandants, Piet Cronje, they climbed the hill up to Massouw's fort and demanded the Chief's immediate surrender. A heated argument ensued – a shot was fired and bloody battle was joined. So fierce was the fray that within minutes ten Boers lay dead.

However, by the end of the Battle of Mamusa, Massouw had suffered a terrible defeat. The Chief himself and all of his counsellors were killed. An extremely unfortunate aspect of the battle was that a large number of women and children were caught up in the crossfire and also perished. The Koranna tribe which, for more than a century, had trekked all the way up from Table Bay, was finally completely destroyed. Fewer than 100 people escaped with their lives that fateful day. They were dispersed among the surrounding tribes and soon lost their identity.

Today the sole reminder of this bloody massacre is the town of Schweizer-Reneke. The name commemorates two of the Transvaal Boers who lost their lives in that battle, Captain C A Schweizer and Veldkornet G N Reneke. Maybe it is time we looked at this place name again and, in the interests of reconciliation, take the other side into consideration.

As for Scotty, the fall of Goshen and Stellaland made very little difference to his life. He remained a law unto himself – nobody could prevent him from going where he wanted to and doing exactly as he pleased.

During Sir Charles Warren's expedition to annex southern Bechuanaland, Scotty was hired as a guide. Shortly after this Scotty purchased a farm and a store in the Kheis area on the Orange, now Senqui, River. But he did no actual farming there. This was merely a cover and a convenient hiding place for stolen stock, before they were re-branded and prepared for market. He acquired a second farm just outside of Amalia village, not very far from Schweizer-Reneke, which he also used for grazing and fattening his purloined cattle. This area is still known as Diewedraai.

A gunrunning exploit of his, into Basutoland, is well worth the telling. In 1871 this country, at the request of King Moshweshwe, had been taken under the protection of the British Crown. But the proud Basuto people had in no sense been conquered. They were still ruled by their King and almost every man possessed a rifle. In 1880, after the Zulu War, the Cape Government, fearing this large force of armed tribesmen, tried to disarm them and many rose in rebellion. The so-called Gun War ensued and, after three years and an expenditure of £4 500 000, it reached an inconclusive end. The rebels were 'defeated', but allowed to retain their weapons, with a strict embargo on new importations. Inevitably, it became the ambition of every Basuto to possess an illicit firearm. They were all prepared to pay a premium and this set of circumstances was just right for our man.

Having secured a large number of Snider rifles, muzzle-loaders and soft-nosed bullets, along with a quantity of powder, Scotty trekked across the Free State, to Ficksburg, near the Basutoland border. He hid his wagons in the bushes close to the road and boldly rode up to the frontier alone. The Veldkornet guarding the border with a handful of men hospitably offered him a cup of coffee. After gaining the man's confidence, Scotty said, 'Look, Meneer. I have some very important information for you. I know that there is a lot of gunrunning taking place, and I have found out that Scotty Smith is the main culprit. What's more, I will show you how he does it! As a matter of fact, I have had a tip that he has just run a cargo into Basutoland, and they have not yet been collected. He's hiding them in a drift on the Caledon River and they are to be collected tonight.'

The officer became very excited. 'Can you show me the place?'

'Yes', Scotty replied. 'It's about twenty kilometres south of here. I don't know if Scotty will still be there, but you had better take all the men you can, as he's a pretty desperate fellow.'

The officer was greatly impressed with the charm of the genial stranger and decided to take no chances. He ordered all his men to mount their horses and, leaving the post to its own devices, they rode hard for a couple of hours to the south. When they came to a drift Scotty and the Veldkornet dismounted and reconnoitred the area. They found no one and the officer ordered the men to picket their horses. They followed Scotty on foot to a bend.

'There!' cried Scotty. 'That's where they are hidden.'

'But surely the powder will spoil in the water?' said the officer.

'Scotty's a sly one', came the reply. 'The boxes will be watertight.'

The men began probing the water and, sure enough, they found one box, then another, then another, but they were too heavy to lift and the entire patrol came to assist. Scotty wandered casually away until he was around the bend, and then ran swiftly to the picketed horses. After setting them loose and stampeding them, he mounted his own steed and galloped back to the border post where he had left his wagons. He quickly inspanned and drove the wagons safely past the deserted border post to the rendezvous deep inside Basutoland.

Meanwhile, the Veldkornet and his men had managed to get some of the enormously heavy boxes to the bank and had prised the lids open, only to find them filled with river boulders. When they looked around for the stranger he had disappeared and so had their horses. They had a long and weary walk back to their post.

Another of his favourite stories concerned an encounter with the Jewish diamond thief. Scotty was transport riding at the time when he happened upon a pedlar walking along the road and offered him a lift. He noticed that the man appeared to be highly agitated and kept glancing over his shoulder.

'What's the matter?' asked Scotty. 'Is something troubling you?'

'It's nothing, it's nothing', the pedlar muttered. They were nearing the border when the man let out a yell.

51

'The police, the police! They are after me!' Scotty turned his head and saw a small posse in the distance.

'Hide me, hide me!' cried the stricken passenger. He flung himself flat on the bed of the wagon and Scotty quickly threw a sail over him and piled some boxes and packages on top.

The police rode up and immediately asked Scotty if he had passed anybody on the road.

'Yes,' replied Scotty, 'I saw a pedlar some way back, if that's the fellow you are after. He's a small man dressed in a dirty corduroy suit and wearing a slouch hat.'

'That's him', cried the Sergeant, 'that's our man alright'.

'What's he done?' asked Scotty.

'Stealing diamonds', came the reply. 'He's got quite a packet on him.'

'Well, if you want to capture him you'll have to retrace your steps. As soon as he saw me coming, he branched off into the veld.'

"Where was that?' the sergeant enquired.

'About four kilometres back there is an ironstone koppie with a small dried-up vlei next to it. That was where I saw him turn off.'

'Thanks!' shouted the Sergeant. 'We'll get him alright. Goodbye!' And he and his men thundered back the way they had come.

At that moment Scotty stuck his hand in his pocket and felt a hard package. A slow grin spread over his face and, stooping down, he whispered to the pedlar, 'I've put the police off the scent, but you had better stay hidden for a while longer.' He opened the parcel and, seeing a number of fairly large diamonds inside, he placed it in one of the wagon boxes. 'It's alright, you can come out now', he called.

The man got out and said, 'Please give me the packet I slipped into your pocket when I thought the police might find me.'

'What packet?' asked Scotty. 'I don't know anything about a packet. You must be making a mistake – look for yourself.' The pedlar ran his hands over Scotty's person but found nothing and, in spite of the man's protestations, he denied all knowledge of the stones. The pedlar kept on wailing, moaning and threatening, until at last Scotty could take no more. He grabbed the man by the shoulders and shouted, 'I've had enough of this nonsense, I hid you from the police and that's all the thanks I get. You accuse me of being a thief! Clear out of here or I'll put a bullet through you, as sure as my name is Scotty Smith!'

A look of horror and fear appeared on the man's face when he realised to whom he had entrusted his precious diamonds and, jumping off the wagon, he ran off across the veld.

Many are the recorded stories of our hero and villain, but there was a side to this cattle thief that touched many hearts, especially women's, in those very harsh times.

During a certain Bloemfontein court case, which Scotty attended – not so much for the court proceedings as for the general information he could pick up from the farmers – he noticed that the Landdrost possessed a particularly fine horse. That evening he slipped into the Landdrost's stables and led the horse out without anybody noticing a thing. He hadn't gone far out of town when it started raining and, soaked to the bone, he knocked on the door of a rather run-down homestead. A woman opened it rather hesitantly.

'Can you put me up for the night?' Scotty enquired.

'I would like to, but my husband isn't here and he made me promise not to admit any strangers while he is away and now I hear that Scotty Smith is in the neighbourhood.'

The older generation, from whom these stories were learnt, told me that when they were children, their parents always used Scotty's name to make them behave. 'If you don't stop that I'll tell Scotty Smith to put you on his saddle and ride away, and you'll never see your poor mommy again!', or words to that effect.

However, on this occasion, Scotty just laughed. 'You have nothing to be afraid of', he said, 'That scoundrel won't show his face while I am here. As a matter of fact, I am after Scotty myself, and the local Landdrost has lent me his personal horse. Don't you recognise it?'

'Yes,' said the woman, 'I know this animal well! I'll give you a room for the night. Take the horse around to the stables whilst I make some supper.'

After they had finished eating they sat and talked for a while and Scotty noticed that his hostess was somewhat sad and distracted.

'What's wrong?' he asked. At first she would not say, but later the story came out.

'I don't know what's going to happen. I told my husband not to do it, but he wouldn't listen to me. He backed a bond for a friend for £200, and now the man has cleared out, and we can't find him anywhere.'

'Don't worry', Scotty comforted her, 'and don't sit up for me either. As soon as the weather clears I'll be off on Scotty's trail.'

He thanked her for her hospitality, paid her, and she retired. Sometime later the storm passed and Scotty got up and rode off into the night. In the morning his hostess rose and went through to the kitchen and there, under a plate on the table, was £200 in bills with a note: 'Best wishes from Scotty Smith.'

Of course the old freebooter did not usually have so much money at his disposal, but he always kept his promises. If he promised a certain farm in the area that their stock would be safe, it was never touched and if he said he would pay for what he called 'borrowed' horses, he always did so, without fail.

Mr David Cowan, a well-known citizen of Victoria West in days gone by, was away on a visit to Beaufort West. A stranger turned up at his house asking for accommodation for the night. His wife was dubious about taking him in, for the usual reasons. But when she confided her fears to the stranger, he laughed. 'You needn't be afraid of Scotty Smith', he said. 'He has never been known to harm a woman.' Mrs Cowan was still rather doubtful but eventually took him in, gave him an outside room and took him his supper. The next morning she sent him some coffee. The maid brought it back. 'The man has gone,' she said, 'but he left a letter on the bed.'

'Thank you for the room and food', it read. 'I am sorry I have had to borrow two of your horses. When your husband returns, tell him to go to the Beaufort West Hotel in ten days time, and he will find them there.'

Mr Cowan did this and found the horses waiting for him at the Hotel.

But it was when it came to befriending the poor and lonely widows in distress that Scotty was in his element. There seems to have been a plentiful supply of poor, lonely and distressed widows in the Orange Free State and western Transvaal at that time. As always, Scotty arrived, looking for a place to sleep and, with his usual tact, had very little difficulty in discovering what the widow's problems were. The farm was bonded and the bondholder was foreclosing the following day. 'How much is the bond?' Scotty asked. '£400' was the reply. Without any hesitation, he dug his hand into his pocket, extracted a thick wad of notes and counted off £400. 'Now, when the man comes tomorrow, you must pay him in full and demand a receipt – that is very important.'

At first the widow demurred and would not accept the money. 'It is quite all right,' said Scotty, 'I will not lose on the deal. You can be sure of that.' She did not understand, but eventually gave way and agreed to do as he said.

The following morning, the bondholder arrived and found, to his great annoyance, that the widow had the money. However, there was nothing he could do about it but give her a receipt and ride away. He had not gone far when, from out of the bushes, appeared a man holding a pistol, who robbed him of all the money he had just received, took his horse from him and galloped away. The following day Scotty visited the farm. The widow was very grateful and asked for his address so that she could eventually repay him. 'Don't worry, the debt has already been settled in full', said the stranger. 'You don't owe me a penny. Goodbye.' And he rode away.

When the First World War broke out in 1914, Scotty Smith was one of the first to offer his services to the Union authorities and was attached to Military Intelligence with the rank of Warrant Officer. Dressed in khaki slacks and shirt, he wandered about, spying on the rebels and reporting their movements and activities to Headquarters.

Soon after war was declared, some of the men who had been Boer leaders during the Anglo-Boer War thought that they now had an opportunity to overthrow British rule in South Africa, and went into open rebellion. Among them were Commandant General C F Beyers, one of the renowned bittereinders, along with General Christian de Wet, whose original farm Roodepoort is now a suburb on the West Rand of Gauteng. His farmhouse, by the way, was the first one burnt in the Transvaal by the British. I have no doubt that General Koos de la Rey would also have joined these rebels, but he had been tragically shot in a roadblock incident in the Johannesburg suburb of Booysens. But that's another story.

In South West Africa, the Germans had concentrated powerful units at Nakop and Raman's Drift, while across the border at Upington and Kakamas were large detachments of the Union Defence Force, under the command of General Manie Maritz, another Anglo-Boer War hero. In October 1914 there was a sensational development. General Maritz deserted to the enemy, taking a large number of men with him. This might have proved a very serious matter, but for some reason, the rebels received very little support from their countrymen. The rising had to be suppressed, however, before Louis Botha could invade South West Africa.

Scotty took part in the invasion of South West Africa, and this story was related by Mr Greeff, who at fifteen had joined the 20th Mounted Rifles (later known as Breytenbach's Light Horse). The campaign took place in the middle of summer, and the sun beat down mercilessly on them. It was not too long before the water carts were empty and, to make matters worse, the commissariat department had broken down and there was no immediate prospect of obtaining fresh supplies.

The position grew more and more critical. In order to spare the horses, the men dismounted and led them. Fortunately, they knew they were near Lutzputs where there were wells of drinking water, and this thought alone kept them going. However, they arrived only to find, to their horror, that one of the wells had dried up and the retiring enemy had polluted the other. A fight had taken place between the rebels and the 8th Mounted, in which the latter had been defeated. The enemy had collected some of the bodies and thrown them into the well before they withdrew. Many of the soldiers were in a state of collapse and the horses were in an even worse plight. The stench from the well was so terrible that the animals refused to drink. One of the men then had a brainwave.

He smeared axle grease up some of the horses' nostrils and in this way gained some relief for the animals, but quite a few actually died of thirst. The officer in charge was desperate and began sending heliograph messages appealing urgently for help.

'Luckily for us', he reported, 'Scotty Smith was in the area and came to our assistance. He arrived at midnight, and we were told to fall in. With Scotty at our head, we set out, leading what remained of the horses, staggering and stumbling through the desert. Fortunately we did not have far to go. Scotty led us straight to the dry bed of the Molopo River. He quickly chose a spot and told us first to picket the horses, then to dig. We had no entrenching tools, so we began excavating a fairly large hole with our hands. The men formed a line and the sand was stuffed into nosebags, and passed along. The sand was soft and before long we were down about a dozen feet. Suddenly one of the men let out a hoarse yell. In a parched, croaking voice he shouted, "Water, boys! Water!" And there, seeping up between the smooth, round river stones, was a thin clear trickle of fresh water. Thank goodness Scotty had had the foresight to picket the horses, otherwise there would have been a stampede.'

True to the tradition of a crack Imperial Cavalry Regiment, these irregular volunteer Union troops looked after the needs of their horses first, before relieving their own thirst.

The year 1919 was a black one for Scotty's admirers all over South Africa. The old veteran contracted influenza and was confined to bed. He became weak but refused to give in. Every now and again a faint smile would cross his lips, as he remembered perhaps something of the full life he had led. Just before his death, he sent a Bushman to call his friend, the priest but, alas, by the time the priest had arrived, Scotty was no longer in need of human sympathy and comfort.

Scotty Smith was buried in the Upington cemetery and a simple metal plaque was erected over his grave. It reads:

George St Leger Gordon Lennox.
Gone but not forgotten. Never will his memory fade.
Wife and Children.

And so South Africa lost one of its folk heroes. Scotty had said to a friend over a fire one night: 'I was born two hundred years too late. You see, my weakness is that, when I see a bunch of good cattle, I want to own them. In modern times this is looked upon as stealing. Two hundred years ago taking other people's cattle in Scotland was known as rieving, and a successful riever was a highly honoured member of his family group. And if the cattle had been rieved from south of the border, the riever was acclaimed a Scottish hero.'

Maybe he had a point.

The Kariega News

Preserved in the Cory Library of Rhodes University in Grahamstown are the last two surviving copies of the newspaper, *The Kariega News*. This is an Eastern Cape story that is well worth the telling, even though the paper, a weekly that ran for just over six months, only ever comprised four pages, had an annual subscription of two shillings and six pence and reached a circulation of only about fifty copies.

Our story starts on Orange Grove, a pretty farm on the Kariega River, some 15 km from Grahamstown. In 1870 it was owned by Lieutenant Charles Bell, who had two sons, the younger of whom, W H Somerset Bell, was fourteen years. His brother Fritz was a year older. Their ambition was to start a newspaper, and so *The Kariega News* was born. When the two young partners had pooled their resources, the total capital of the venture amounted to five shillings in cash and a regular income, if the boys did their chores at home, of threepence a week. This, they felt, was sufficient to launch their careers as aspirant newspaper magnates.

Somerset Bell set out for Grahamstown with the entire capital of the business. He was able to purchase two pounds of second-hand long printer's type and he and his brother manufactured the rest of the printing apparatus themselves. By mixing lamp black and linseed oil in the proportions obtained from an old recipe in an encyclopaedia, they produced printer's ink and, using an old roll of ceiling paper found in the loft, they went to print. There was only enough type for one page, so each time a new page was to be printed, the type had to be reset and each page placed separately under the press. When they ran short of a particular letter, they altered the last paragraphs of the page accordingly.

The amazing thing is that the youthful Somerset Bell has left us a complete record of how the printing was done. Suffice to say that by using such things as a piece of flat duct iron, the back of a fire-grate, and a leaf from a mahogany table, this triumph of ingenuity was accomplished.

The first number of *The Kariega News* appeared on 12 September 1870 and many subscribers, aware of the boys' brave effort, paid their annual half crowns in advance, thereby augmenting the enterprise's capital base. This enabled newer and better equipment to be obtained and the standard of the publication improved dramatically.

Like true professionals, the two newspapermen announced that they had secured an exclusive scoop – news from the Franco-Prussian war front would be published regularly. The letters were actually written to Lieutenant Bell from the front by a family friend, Dr H S Taylor, who accompanied the Prussian army during the conquest of France.

And so the paper prospered and its fame spread far beyond the Kariega River. A Mr William Dewey from the town of Alice, who founded a newspaper called *The Chumie Banner,* wrote to ask the boys for advice on how to acquire a small printing press.

Being entirely unaware of the law of libel, they published an anonymous letter sent to the newspaper, referring in rather sneering terms to the habits of one of the new arrivals in Grahamstown. They soon received a missive from Mr J Montague Stone, a well-known Grahamstown attorney, demanding the name of the author of the letter, an apology and payment of costs, or £200 in damages. They immediately ran to their father for help and, taking his advice, they published Mr Stone's letter with an addendum saying that they hoped that the author of the anonymous letter would correspond directly with Mr Stone. Fortunately the matter rested there and no more was heard.

But the days of *The Kariega News* were numbered. Their father, Charles Bell, was appointed resident magistrate at Leribe in Lesotho and the two budding newspaper magnates were bundled off to boarding school at St Andrews College. On 4 April 1871, with sad hearts, they published the last issue of *The Kariega News*. The printing press was dismantled and, like true businessmen, they sold it for a profit to Mr Dewey in Alice.

So, this incredible venture in youthful initiative and enterprise drew to a close. But people like that are not kept down for long. Somerset became a lawyer in Grahamstown, subsequently building up a big practice in Kimberley and then Johannesburg. In 1896, he was a member of the Reform Committee which invited Dr Jameson to invade the Transvaal. He was arrested along with others such as Sir Abe Bailey and Percy Fitzpatrick and lodged in Pretoria prison, eventually released with a fine of £2 000.

However, I don't think anything ever gave him a bigger thrill than when, at the age of fourteen, he stood in Grahamstown holding in his hands the first copy of *The Kariega News*.

The wreck of the St. John and the St. Jerome

The first recorded shipwrecks on the South African coast occurred in 1552. The *St. John* and the *St. Jerome* had left Cochin in the East and were sailing for Portugal. Both were very heavily laden, the *St. John* being heaviest, as she was the biggest galleon in the Eastern trade at that time. They sailed together without incident until they reached the east coast of South Africa and a south-easterly wind tore into them. They turned tail and ran before this hurricane, which then veered suddenly to the north-west.

The *St. Jerome*'s send came just north of the Umhlatuzi River (the forceful one), a little to the south of what came to be named Richards Bay. Beyond some flotsam and jetsam and wreckage dumped on the beach, she left no human survivors to tell her tale.

The *St. John,* dismasted and badly damaged, turned and ran southwards before the storm until 8 June 1552, when the crew finally managed to anchor in the vicinity of the Mthamvuna River, at present-day Port St John's, named after the galleon. Here they managed to land and spent three days conveying the people and cargo to the safety of the shore. They intended to run the galleon ashore at some appropriate place, dismantle her and with her timbers construct a caravel, in which they hoped to sail to Inhambane, then the nearest town, for this all took place 100 years before Van Riebeeck landed at the Cape. However, on the fourth night another fierce winter storm struck, flinging the galleon onto the rocks as if it had been a straw. One hundred and ten people were drowned and merchandise to the value of a million cruzados was buried at sea.

The survivors, numbering a little more than 500 (300 of whom were slaves), gathered in tents upon the beach. It was decided to divide into three groups and on 7 July, after a bit of local trading, they set off on the long walk up the coast to Mozambique, a distance, with deviations, of about 1 000 km. The expedition started boldly enough, with members of the crew carrying the wealthier passengers, who had the necessary means of payment. But as they travelled, fording rivers, pushing through sand, sleeping miserably in the rain and cold with scant food, people began to fall by the wayside. The first to go were the sick and then the weaklings and the rich, whose way of life had made them flabby and whose money now counted for nothing.

The company pressed on, fording those dozens of South Coast rivers, up the entire length of Natal. Local Africans snatched what pickings they could and a grim train of camp followers walked close behind – jackals and hyenas cleaning up the human debris.

Finally, in October 1552, some three months after being shipwrecked, 200 survivors stumbled into the kraal of the kindly Chief Nyaka, on the Bay of Mozambique. The other 300-odd souls had either found release from suffering in death, or had stayed to pour a variety of Asiatic and European blood into the veins of the descendants of the tribespeople who gave them welcome sanctuary along the way. Sufficiently rested, the survivors then pushed northwards towards Imhambane, the nearest European trading settlement.

Manuel de Sousa de Sepulveda, the Captain of the *St. John,* was a Portuguese nobleman of refinement and renown, and was accompanied by his highborn wife Dona Leonora and their two small children. Dona Leonora and the children had survived the journey to this point, but with hindsight, it might have been better had they gone down with the galleon. They came upon a tribe of hostile people who surrounded their little band and demanded that Dona Leonora be stripped of all her clothing. It is said that Dona Leonora fought them off with blows, as she preferred to die than to stand naked in front of these tribesmen. Her life would have ended right there had it not been for the intervention of Manuel de Sousa, who begged her to allow herself to be stripped, reminding her that it is the will of God that we are all born naked. So, while her children stood around her weeping, Dona Leonora allowed herself to be stripped naked.

She covered herself with her long hair and burrowed a pit in the sand, where she buried herself up to the waist, and never rose from that position again. Her children refused to leave her and they died of exposure in the cruel tropical sun, while her husband wandered off into the bush to die.

Of the rest of the company, some twenty-two in total eventually reached Inhambane, where a trading vessel found them some time later and ransomed them from the Africans for two pence farthing per person, and in this way the entire, terrible story of their epic journey was preserved.

What we fail to remember, I believe, is that the *St. John* was a slaver, that the local tribes recognised some of the crew, and that what they did to them was but a small revenge for the misery that the trade in human flesh had caused amongst the Mozambique tribes. For Dona Leonora was never touched, she was just left to die.

The footprint in Mpumalanga

Near the southern tip of Africa, there are still unknown places, places that defy our knowledge and play games with our senses and beliefs, places that are sacred to the local inhabitants and of which we know dangerously little. One such place is situated in a forest on the eastern side of Mpumalanga. It consists of two special hills about three kilometres apart. I was privileged to be taken there by an old Zulu sanusi, that is, the 'high priest' of sangomas, the one who trains others in the craft.

Accompanying us on our laborious climb up the hill was a Hopi Indian shaman, whose totem was the eagle. We sat on the hillside and the shaman began to chant. I felt quite embarrassed, having a Red Indian hopping around and yelling his traditional chant. But soon my embarrassment turned into astonishment and the hairs on my arm rose. The air appeared to become charged and it pulsated all around us, with an inwards and outwards movement. I looked up into the sky and there, coming over the ridge, was a pair of black eagles, flying towards us as if they had been summoned. High over our heads they soared, once, twice and then slowly disappeared in the direction from which they had come. The shaman stopped chanting and I saw that the old sanusi was in a deep trance.

Gesturing down the hillside, the sansui drew my attention to a massive boulder, one that, when I looked at it, appeared strangely out of place with its surroundings. 'According to our beliefs', he told me, 'this rock was brought and placed here by the ancient peoples, who would come and conduct ceremonies and prayers at this most holy site.' When I enquired why this particular place was holy, he rose up and led me gently down the hill, and there, behind the boulder, I was shown 'The Footprint'.

Imprinted in solid rock, embedded about 20 cm deep, was a perfect imprint of a human being's left foot. One can see clearly all the individual toemarks, looking just like that of someone who had walked over wet beach sand, from the way the toes had gripped and scoured the sand. I could see the ball of the foot, the raised portion of the instep, and the heel. Nothing too unusual there – except that the footprint is just under 2 m in length, the footprint of a giant, approximately 11 m tall!

The footprint has defied all expert analysis. Baffled geologists have put forward different opinions, some saying that it is too perfect to be caused by natural weathering, others saying it's a natural footprint left in the sands hundreds of thousands of years ago, before it solidified into rock. If you look closely at the imprint, you will notice that the big toe is firmly tucked into the the rest of the toes. This is an indication that the owner did not spend all his – or her – time barefooted, as the big toe in such a person splays out from the rest of the toes for balance.

'To whom did this footprint belong?' I enquired respectfully of the sanusi. He replied that the local legends refer to the owner as the 'Heavenly Princess' – and that the only reference the white people have is that part of the Judeo-Christian Bible which refers to the time when giants walked upon the Earth.

The old sanusi then pointed across the valley, to the opposite hillside. 'This hill is also considered a sacred place by our people. Many years before', he told me, 'a white man with long black hair came riding down on the back of an unknown animal. He wore a skin of iron and had slits for eyes.' I immediately recognised that he was referring to a man dressed in a suit of armour, riding upon a horse which was, of course, unknown to the old black people. 'The man carried a sword strapped to his side', the sanusi continued. He was known as 'Juanna'. Juanna, was greatly feared by the local people, and they decided to kill him as quickly as possible. They persuaded his young, impressionable black aide to betray him. And so, in the middle of the night the aide crept up upon Juanna as he slept, took his sword and threw it deep into the forest. He then gave the signal and the people fell upon Juanna and killed him.

What the old man was unaware of was that, by the purest coincidence, I was at that time researching an extraordinary historical figure. He was known as 'Prester John' and, to this day, historians know very little about him. What we do know is that he was a European adventurer of the 15th century, and that he spent many years exploring Africa. Prester John had written to various Kings of Europe, telling them about the enormous wealth of gold and silver in Africa and also offering his personal armies to help them in war. Nothing more was ever heard from him and he disappeared without trace.

The search for Prester John became something of a crusade in the 15th century – particularly for a group of men who called themselves 'The Knights of Christ'. The Knights of Christ were, in a way, successors to the Knights Templar, a holy order of warrior Knights, who had led the capture of Jerusalem during the Crusades. What exactly the Knights Templar found in digging under the Dome of the Rock is not known, but what we do know is that they fell out with the Pope at Rome. He excommunicated them, stripped them of much of their property and many were killed. But Portugal found a novel way of keeping the Templars alive. They were disbanded to appease the Pope and 'The Knights of Christ' immediately came into being, inheriting the lands and wealth of the Templars.

The Knights of Christ wore the red Maltese cross emblazoned across their chests. The great voyagers, such as Vasco da Gama (and also his patron, Henry the Navigator) were all Knights of Christ. When Vasco da Gama set out from Portugal, it was not only to discover the sea-route around the tip of Africa. His brief was also to search for the elusive Prester John. The Portuguese name for John is Juan, very close to what the Africans called the man in armour.

An entry in Vasco da Gama's ship's log mentions that when he anchored off the coast of what is now Mozambique, the local tribes told

67

him that 'Juanna' was in the hinterland. Da Gama became extremely excited by this and sent out a search party to make contact, but to no avail. Despondently he returned to Portugal.

Is it just possible that the final resting place of this enigmatic character, Prester John, lies at the foot of this most sacred hill? Maybe someday we will know.

Today, in the city of Port Elizabeth, there stands a monument near the City Hall, which was erected by the Portuguese government. It is dedicated to all those brave Portuguese seafarers who risked life and limb – in the search for Prester John!

The old Sanusi was tired. He had made, in his old age, his last visit to the holy place and it was time to go. A million questions were racing around in my head, but my better judgement told me to leave the subject alone, and keep what I had learned and experienced to myself.

Modjadji

Should you stand on the top of Pypkop Ridge near Duiwelskloof and cast your eyes over the forest-clad folds of the Walowedu Mountains, you would be gazing at the ancient lands of Modjadji – 'The Transformer of the Clouds' – 'She who must be obeyed'. And as you stand and watch the mists and the greenery of those ancient mountains, you have to keep blinking, for you tend to slip away into an ancient time, a time in which Rider Haggard immortalised a Queen called 'She'.

It is told in the legends that there was a time long ago when there were no people in this part of the world, only the beasts of the forest. The hoarse bark of the baboons, the soft sighing of the winds, and the roar of tumbling waters, were the only sounds. All the people lived away to the north, in 'Monomotaba'. Among those tribes there was one whose priests told of their origins near 'the great waters that had no end'. These priests and chieftains wore around their necks, blue beads, the sacred 'Uhulungu ha madi' or 'beads of the sea' – the emblem of royalty and relics of a culture possibly older than that of the Phoenicians.

And in the forest depths, parents told their children tales of fierce warriors and ancient cities, and a lost race who lived in the land of their forefathers – a white race, whiter than the Arab slavers who pillaged their cities. But time and the bush had swallowed this race of white people, and the people of the blue beads were called the 'BaVenda' – 'people of the world'.

69

One day there came from West Africa a warlike tribe, pillaging and looting, and the people were forced to flee southwards to the mountains now called the Walowedu. Amongst the tribes who fled were the 'Lovedu', led by a woman who, it was said, was a white woman. Her name was Modjadji.

Who was this woman? Was she the daughter of some captive white woman, or of one of the tribes from that far-off land near the waters that have no end? Was she the descendant of some noble house, with the blood of Semitic kings in her veins? Or was she a waif, thrown up on some remote slave market? Modjadji, on the rocky heights, her priests guarding her from prying eyes, and weaving an aura of mysticism and dread power of the spirit world around her, to such effect that, when the white people arrived, they called the area Duiwelskloof – 'The Valley of the Devils'.

It was said that Modjadji's lovers were either killed or became her slaves and that her male offspring were all put to death. Only a female child, who had to be conceived incestuously, could inherit the mantle of tribal rule. Whatever the land and people who bore her, Modjadji had the blood of conquerors in her veins and, as her tribesmen were not great warriors, it was by the fairness of her body, the cunning of her mind and the savagery of her heart, that she created and moulded a great kingdom out of the tribes who settled in that area.

So great was the fame of this sorceress that chiefs of the Basuto, the Shangaans and others came to pay her homage and bought gifts of young girls as handmaidens to the queen. Even Shaka, the great Zulu king, who feared no man, dreaded the magical powers of Modjadji and sent a deputation headed by Dumisa, his own personal sangoma, to propitiate the Rain Queen.

When Modjadji reached old age, she would announce her successor and retire into a cave, take a special type of poison made from the spine of the Ngwenya (crocodile) and then die alone. Her people believed that she was immortal and that her spirit entered into the younger female, thereby ensuring a continuous reign. What we do know is that the whiteness of her skin slowly, over generations, grew darker and darker.

Then in 1894, came the white man, with guns.

Modjadji suffered her first major setback at the hands of Commandant-General Piet Joubert of the Zuid-Afrikaansche Republiek, and the reigning Modjadji died by her own hand, after the Commandant had broken her power.

It is said that until then, no white person had ever seen Modjadji and the old woman who shuffled out and spoke to Piet Joubert was a fake. The real Modjadji had been taken away to safety. The tribe was severely punished for deceiving General Joubert and later the real Modjadji was dragged into his presence. After this ignominy, she took poison, and died the ritual death of her ancestors.

The present Modjadji still resides in that area, but receives visitors and can be seen in her kraal by all and sundry. A strange and interesting rider to this story is that the latest DNA testing has proved that the Lemba – a subgroup of the BaVenda, do actually spring from Semitic stock – makes one wonder doesn't it?

'Isivavani'

It seems a pity that, as we go barrelling along the now computerized highway of an ever-faster lifestyle, many of the old ways, customs and facts about this, our ancient land, have disappeared and been forgotten, lost in the mists of time.

Take for instance the fact that many of our older roads follow the ancient game trails that once covered the country, for example, the old road that links Empangeni to Durban, the Great North Road into the interior and the old road from Pretoria to Rustenburg, to mention but a few. All these roads were built upon the seasonal migratory tracks of the elephants. The reason is actually quite simple and logical, for the elephant, being the largest creature on dry land, has the inborn ability to seek out the easiest route across any terrain, including through the mountains. So, for the ancient peoples travelling on foot, it made sense to follow these paths. Then arrived the wagons, which followed the footpaths, and so there evolved dirt roads and, finally, tarred roads.

As you drive along these older roads, you will notice that they twist and turn, sometimes for no apparent reason. Possibly an elephant long ago uprooted a tree along the way. The path was then simply made to go around it and the road still curves, though the tree has long since rotted away. Many people think these kinks in the road were because of land-holdings, but the laying out of the farms came very much later.

Along some of these oldest dirt roads, usually at crossroads, you may still come across a cairn of stones piled high by the roadside. These have a special significance in the history of our peoples and are called in Zulu, 'isivavani'.

In times gone by, when a man had to embark upon a journey of importance, he would bid farewell to his family and the kraal and proceed along the road towards his destination. At the first crossroads he came to he would stop, look around and find a suitably sized stone, close his eyes and hold the stone to his forehead. He would then make two wishes. The first would be for the travellers who had preceded him upon this road, hoping that their journey had been a happy one, as well as successful. The next wish would be made for the travellers following him. He would then place the stone on the pile at the side of the road. You will notice that, in this most ancient ritual, he did not make a wish for himself. According to the belief of Ubuntu, your needs are covered by the people who have gone before you, as well as by those who will follow.

So these 'isivavani' are a very special part of our heritage. They should be respected and preserved, and their significance explained to future generations, so that that their meaning may be carried forward.

On one occasion, people who were not aware of the importance of these cairns found what they saw as a handy pile of stones next to the Mzinyathi River. They were in the process of re-interring the remains of Lieutenants Melvill and Coghill, British soldiers killed while trying to save the Queen's colour of the 24th Regiment after the battle of Isandlwana. They removed the stones and built them into the new graves. To the white people's horror and dismay, the local people 'desecrated' the graves by removing the stones. It took the owner of the farm, David Rattray, to discover the root cause. It just serves to show how much we all still have to learn about differences in our country's cultures.

The wreck of
the *Doddington*

People who have been to Port Elizabeth will probably know Bird Island, which lies north-west of the city, across the Algoa Bay and off the coast of a place now called Woody Cape. However, not many are aware of a submerged rock, called 'Doddington Rock', which lies just south-west of Bird Island. The *African Pilot,* a publication of the British Admiralty, states the following:

> Between and around these rocks and islands, the depth is irregular, and in bad weather, a heavy sea rolls over the whole area, breaking in from 8 to 10 fathoms to the seaward of the group. In heavy weather, a vessel should not approach them in less than 60 fathoms.

The Captain of the East Indiaman *Doddington,* unfortunately, did not have a copy of these instructions when, at 12:45 a.m. on 17 July 1755, she passed the entrance to Algoa Bay. William Webb, the ship's third mate, kept a diary which tells how he was woken as the ship struck the rock. It was in heavy seas and the rock split her hull like a butcher's cleaver.

She broke up in a matter of hours and the survivors made for Bird Island in the pitch darkness. Of the 270 souls aboard, just twenty-three made it to the island, a desolate, barren speck of land, where they could anticipate only death from thirst and starvation. But as the day broke, they began to take courage – stores were being washed onto the island's shore and they collected necessities such as flour, casks of water, salted

74

pork, barrels of brandy, rolls of sailcloth, canvas, candles, seven live pigs, gun flints and even dry gunpowder. They started to build a camp. A couple of days later, three iron-banded chests were found. Some of the treasures from India, hundreds of thousands of pounds in gold and coin, had been washed up.

The story I am about to tell you was researched by the late Frank Cooper, one of the Port Elizabeth's Library's most professional maritime researchers. It remains one of South Africa's queerest treasure tales.

On that day in 1755, when the castaways saw the ironbound chests lying on the beach, something changed. Till then everyone had got on extremely well and they had even commenced laying the keel of the sloop that they were going to build from the flotsam. The chests had been placed under the charge of an officer, but some while later a disturbing discovery was made. One of the chests had been forced open and the contents removed. All were paraded before Evan Jones, the first mate (the Captain had drowned in the wreck). However, as was the law in those days, being bereft of a ship, they were no longer under the oath of obedience and the officers had no authority over them. No one stepped forward and the matter had to be dropped.

Work progressed on the sloop and on 17 February 1756 the *Happy Deliverance,* as she was named, set sail for Delagoa Bay. Aboard her were all their remaining stores, including kegs of water, seabird eggs and the remains of the treasure. They put in at places along the coast to barter for food and, sixty-one days after leaving the island (their last act before leaving had been to christen it Bird Island), they sailed triumphantly into Delagoa Bay. There were anchored two English trading vessels, the *Rose* and the *Snow,* belonging to Captain Chandler. It is recorded that Chandler bought the *Happy Deliverance* for 500 rupees and the three vessels sailed in company to Bombay. What happened to the stolen treasure remained a mystery – it definitely was not on the sloop.

The scene now shifts to Cape Town in 1757, where a Dutchman, Gerrit van Bengal, was sitting in a waterfront tavern drinking and talking to two sailors. They turned out to be survivors of the wreck of the *Doddington* and related the following tale.

They had taken one of the surviving small boats to go fishing and had strayed too close to the back line of the waves. The boat capsized. One of their mates was drowned, but they managed to reach the shore of Woody Cape, then called Kwaaihoek. In a cave near the waterfront they said they distinctly saw ironbound chests half-buried in the sand. The boat had been washed ashore and, agreeing not to say a word about their find, they rowed back to Bird Island. Unfortunately, the *Happy Deliverance* was completed before they could get back to the beach at Kwaaihoek and they sailed away, never to return. Gerrit van Bengal managed to obtain a passage on the *Zwaardfisch* which anchored off Bird Island during bad weather. By offering a share of the treasure, he managed to persuade three crew members to row him ashore. However, the place was not called Kwaaihoek for nothing. The boat capsized in the surf and Gerrit managed to hold on to the keel and was washed up on the shore. The other three men drowned.

Undaunted, he recognised the place from the description given to him and there he found a Dutch blunderbuss, along with an old cutlass, heavy with rust. He hunted and dug around for days but found nothing more. The ship, presuming the men all drowned, sailed away and Gerrit van Bengal began the 1 000 km walk back to Cape Town.

Upon arrival he went to Governor Ryk Tulbagh and told him the story. The Governor was sceptical. But Gerrit had become obsessed with the tale and the Cape authorities, thinking he had gone mad, sent him back to Holland. Upon arrival, he wrote the adventure down. He then slowly lost his mind and eventually ended his days in an asylum.

Nearly 100 years later, Advocate Simeon Proof found the manuscript in a second-hand hand bookshop, and edited and published the pamphlet which he entitled, *Singular adventures of Gerrit van Bengal, principally on the South East Coast of the Cape of Good Hope in the years 1748 to 1758*. Copies are extremely rare as they were published in Holland in 1860.

There is a curious aftermath to the tale, for in 1824, more than sixty years after the wreck, a Jan Trichard of the farm Olifantshoek, not far from Woody Cape, discovered a huge iron treasure chest on the beach.

He hurried back to the homestead, blurted out the news to his wife and son and took a span of oxen to the beach. While his attention was concentrated on inspanning the oxen to pull the box out, a massive wave engulfed both him and the span and, barring his son who was a safe distance away, all were washed out to sea. The place was not called Kwaaihoek for nothing. The box was never seen again.

The well-known diver, Dave Allen, dived there during the 1970s and was able to identify the *Doddington* wreck from the large quantity of 'pieces of eight' that matched the official ship's manifest in England. But as for the chests in the sand, nothing has ever come to light – maybe, like the *Grosvenor*, which was elusive for so long, its time is drawing near!

The legend of Hendrik Schoeman

Hendrik Schoeman owned the farm 'Schoemans Rust', adjacent to the now historical monument 'Groot Plaas' once owned by the famous Andries Pretorius. Schoemansrust is today the site of the Hartebeestpoort Dam in Gauteng. As a young man Schoeman had fought in the First Anglo-Boer War of 1880–81 and, as a Commandant, proved both his bravery and his loyalty to the Zuid-Afrikaansche Republiek (ZAR). He was the commander in charge of the siege of Pretoria that kept the British pinned down so effectively, and was an acclaimed Afrikaner hero.

With the outbreak of the Second Anglo-Boer War in 1899, Schoeman once again served his country. However, when Bloemfontein, the capital of the Orange Free State, fell, followed shortly by Pretoria, capital of the ZAR, Schoeman argued that the British were deadly serious about the Oath of Neutrality and, to prevent hardship and the deaths of the Boer women and children, it would be better if the Boers surrendered. The ultimatum came from Field-Marshal Lord Roberts on 10 June 1900, that infamous statement which was to cause such bitter and abiding hatred between the English and the Afrikaner, surviving even to this day. The ultimatum read:

> If the Boer forces do not surrender and sign the Oath of Neutrality, we will raze their farms to the ground, remove all food and livestock, and intern the women, children and farmhands in internment camps.

78

The prospect of such destruction distressed Schoeman and he warned his colleagues of the terrible fate that would befall the nation. He stopped fighting, went to Pretoria, and signed the Oath. The British, true to their word, allowed him to return to his farm Schoemansrust.

The Boers were so incensed by this that a commando arrived on Schoeman's farm and arrested him on a charge of high treason. Jan Smuts was the Attorney-General of the Transvaal at the time and, upon reviewing the charges, he refused to prosecute, saying that they could not be seen at this juncture to be prosecuting their own heroes. Smuts sent him, under guard, to General Louis Botha who was fighting east of Pretoria, along the Delagoa Bay railway line.

Botha was so disgusted with what Schoeman had done that he immediately re-arrested him on a charge of high treason. He was tried in Barberton, but acquitted and allowed to go back to his farm. However, fate had not nearly finished with this man. He had been away from his farm for nearly three months and the British, suspecting that he had reneged on his Oath, burnt his farm to the ground, looted his cattle and completely destroyed all he possessed.

Broken in spirit and dejected, he returned to his house in Boom Street, Pretoria, and there he sat on the stoep and watched as his worst nightmare took place before his very eyes. The Boer women and children were being herded into concentration camps all over the Transvaal, Natal and Orange Free State, at Middelburg, Klerksdorp, Winburg and Irene, to name but a few. By October 1901 there were some 120 000 people in those camps, and conditions were far from sanitary. By the end of that war, well over 20 000 people had died in the camps, mainly from diseases such as typhoid, dysentery and measles.

So distraught did Schoeman become in witnessing this terrible tragedy befalling his people that he mounted his horse and galloped into the Magaliesburg, where the 'bittereinder' Generals, De La Rey and Beyers, were still fighting on. He intercepted Beyers at Sterkstroom, and pleaded with him, for the sake of the women and children, to surrender. The British troops numbered in excess of 400 000 and the Boers not many more than 80 000. Beyers would not listen to the old man. He had him arrested him and thrown into gaol, this time in Pietersburg, in what is now the Northern Province. There he stayed until Colonel Plummer captured Pietersburg in April 1901.

Schoeman returned to his house in Pretoria, where he came to a sad end. An old artillery shell, that he had kept from his First Boer War campaign days, was set off by a spark from the fireplace and exploded, killing him and his eldest daughter. There is an urban legend that the Boers actually killed him, for the 'bittereinders' could not stand the 'hensoppers', but we shall never know for sure.

Nevertheless, the townsfolk from the little village that had sprung up on the far side of the Hartebeestpoort Dam had a large memorial stone cross erected upon a hill, overlooking the place where his farmhouse had been, and there it stands to this day. The inscription tells how very hard it must have been to be so prophetic, but yet be rejected by your own people.

The Adam Kok trek

The story of how the Griqua lost their land at Philippolis in the aftermath of the Great Trek is a story of British betrayal. The Griqua were loyal to the British authority at the Cape. What many of us are not aware of, because emphasis is always placed on the white Trek, is the fact that there were many separate treks, all involving people of colour. Certainly, the trek of the Griqua under their leader Adam Kok was one of the epics of the 19th century.

When it suited the British they repudiated treaties and made a virtual present of an ally's territory to that ally's enemy.

Adam Kok II died in September 1835, on the way home from trying in vain to persuade the Governor of the Cape to sign a treaty similar to the one with Andries Waterboer at Griquatown. He had been equally unsuccessful in persuading the Governor to take effective action to stop white trekkers from flooding into his country. To cut a very long and complicated story short, the Griqua eventually found themselves facing the following unpalatable alternatives. Either the British would annex their lands or their lands would be annexed by the trekkers, returning from across the Drakensberg, as a result of the British annexation of Natal. The tension between the leader of the returning trekkers, one Mocke, and the Griqua was so high that Mocke placed himself under Hendrik Potgieter when the Boers attacked the Griqua at Philippolis. In this battle one Griqua and ten Boers were killed. Two regiments were sent up from the Cape to retrieve 2 000 Griqua cattle from the trekkers.

81

Sir Harry Smith then repudiated the old treaty, told Adam Kok III that he was going to take his land away and threatened to hang him on the spot.

It was then that the Griqua decided to trek from Philippolis and because this was a coloured trek, the event has until recently been denied its rightful place in our history. More than 2 000 people, 300 wagons and carts and 20 000 head of cattle and sheep set out on a journey that would take them over two years. They would have to blast their way through the mountains and trek over the Malutis to a place then called Nomansland, lying between the Transkei to the south and Natal to the north. First, however, they had to sell their farms in Philippolis, and obtain permission from Moshweshwe to trek through Basutoland.

The first Griqua trekkers left towards the end of 1860 and established a base near the modern Zastron, where the rest of the trekkers joined them. They had decided to wait another winter before trekking on, but this was a disastrous decision as the winter of 1862 was extremely severe and a year of drought nearly ruined them. Their cattle and sheep died by the thousands and vultures circled continuously overhead.

When the spring came they pressed ahead, blasting a way through the mountains to the very source of the Orange or Gariep River. Eventually, after the loss of many animals and wagons in steep ravines, they dragged themselves over Ongeluksnek in the summer of 1862–63, and descended into their Promised Land. They founded Griqualand East, but little did they realise at the time that, having endured such hardship, it would be barely fifteen years before the land that they had called their own, with the blessings of the British authorities, would be annexed by Britain.

Today Kokstad, the capital of Griqualand East, still bears reference to the name of their leader, Adam Kok.

Prince Louis Napoleon

In a rather isolated, flat piece of veld near the road between Melmoth and Vryheid in Kwazulu-Natal, stands a monument marking the place where Louis Napoleon, the Prince Imperial and the last of the Napoleons, met his end, in June 1879 during the course of the Anglo-Zulu War. He was just twenty-three years old. His father, Napoleon III, and his mother, Princess Eugenie, had sought refuge in England after the Franco-Prussian War of 1870–71 when Napoleon III was forced to abdicate and France became a Republic. After some persuasion by Queen Victoria, Prince Louis was allowed to study at the Woolwich Military Academy where, at the age of nineteen, he qualified as an Artillery Officer in the British Army, passing out top of his class in horsemanship and fencing.

The British had invaded Zululand and, after the ignominious defeat suffered at Isandlwana, Lord Chelmsford had called for reinforcements from Britain. Many of the Prince's fellow officers had been called up and, wanting to show gratitude to the British and wishing even more to redeem the name of Napoleon in France, the young man saw a brilliant opportunity in the Zulu War. Princess Eugenie was dead against the idea, as was the British Prime Minister, Benjamin Disraeli. But Queen Victoria again intervened and it was agreed that, being a foreigner, he could not be sent overseas as an officer, but would be allowed to go as an 'observer'. Lord Chelmsford had mightier issues on his mind. When Louis Napoleon arrived in Durban, he, along with Lieutenant Jahleel

Carey, were placed under Quartermaster Colonel Harrison, the officer in charge of reconnaissance. Jahleel Carey had been educated in France and he and the Prince got along very well.

Carey asked permission from Colonel Harrison to accompany Louis Napoleon on a sketching trip into an area that the scouts had reported, was free of Zulus. Permission was granted and, along with six mounted troops and a friendly Zulu as a guide, they set out on the morning of 1 June 1879. The English accounts tell us that they came across a deserted kraal that afternoon, they unsaddled and brewed some tea. A Zulu impi came out of the long grass and fell upon them. In the firing, shouting, and general melee, two troopers and the Zulu guide were cut off from their horses and were killed. There was pandemonium as the rest tried to mount and run. Napoleon's horse reared and bolted and Napoleon, holding onto the carbine holster, was dragged some 100 metres before the strap holding the holster broke. He slipped and fell under the horse.

Lieutenant Carey managed to gather the rest of the party and, realising that it would be disastrous to return with five men as the area was overrun with Zulus, he hotfooted it back to Itelezi camp.

Louis Napoleon had ventured forth accompanied by only eight men. More than a thousand men went to look for his body. All the British cavalry was there, together with all the mounted volunteers and the Edendale members of the Natal Native Contingent. When they searched the area the following day, they found Trooper Abel, killed by a bullet from a captured British carbine, and Trooper Rogers, who had been killed with spears, propped up against a bank, his eyes open and face frozen in an expression of shock. Further away, in a donga, lay the body of Louis Napoleon, naked except for a gold wristlet and a necklace containing his father's miniature.

The news shook the world. It received more coverage than the Isandlwana defeat and the French, who for years had felt nothing for Napoleon III or his family, were up in arms in a frenzy of Anglophobia. It is said that Queen Victoria, upon receiving the news, did not sleep for two days. In typical British fashion at that time, a scapegoat had to be found, and this role fell to Lieutenant Carey. He was court-martialled in

Durban, found guilty of misbehaviour in the face of the enemy and sent home at once. Lord Chelmsford intended to have him cashiered, but Princess Eugenie, eschewing revenge, appealed on his behalf to Queen Victoria, who intervened and Carey was reprieved. He later joined the Indian Army, where, after bearing the contempt of his fellow officers for a few years and, having become totally ruined with no prospect of advancement, the burden became too great and he committed suicide.

All of Natal bowed their heads in 1880 as the grief-stricken Eugenie slowly made her way up into Zululand, visiting all the battlefields and, finally, the donga where her only son had died. The party found Subuza, who owned the kraal nearby. She bought the site from him and planted a willow sapling and an ivy shoot there. Then she returned to England.

We should also listen to what the Zulus have to say about this incident. Yes, they agree, a patrol of British did come to Subuza's Kraal, and, yes, there were no men there as they were away serving in the 'Magoba Mkosi' ('Benders of the Kings') impi. But the Zulu maidens were there in the kraal and Napoleon, with his good looks and obviously regal bearing, was quite attractive. Zulu tradition tells us that there were a few dalliances that afternoon, that the 'Magoba Mkosi' regiment, upon returning, came across this scene and that it was then that the massacre occurred.

What the real story is, we will never know, but the Zulus have nothing to hide, so why not tell it as it was?

The first Cape Slave Revolt

A t the time of the Second British Occupation of the Cape in 1806,
there were 29 800 slaves and 22 600 colonists. The British then
passed a law prohibiting the importation of more slaves, but
nothing was done about the slaves still in service. By the time slavery
was abolished in 1834, there were some 40 000 slaves in the Cape alone.
It is in that period – between the second British Occupation in 1806 and
slave emancipation in 1834 that there were two slave revolts.

The first slave revolt in 1808 was very strange indeed. Its two chief
instigators were a labourer named James Hooper and an Irish sailor,
Michael Kelly. The Irish were much abused by the British at that time.

James Hooper had arrived some months earlier and had taken
lodgings with a slave named Louis, who was married to a free woman.
His owner allowed him to live and work in town in exchange for some
of his earnings. The men began swapping grievances and were soon
plotting the general emancipation of the slaves and the overthrow of the
Cape Government.

The plan was to rally the slaves in the outlying farm districts around
Malmesbury and then march into Cape Town, where they expected to be
joined by the town slaves, all demanding their freedom. If it were
refused, they would seize the prison and powder magazine, and fight for
it. Confident of success, they voted Louis to be the new head of state.

They didn't stand a chance. They overestimated their ability to rally
the slaves and underestimated the 5 000-odd soldiers garrisoned in Cape

Town. Michael Kelly, along with two others, Abraham and Adonis, joined the force. Hooper and Abraham rode on horseback to the farm of Pieter Louw in the Malmesbury district to obtain promises of support from the slaves. On obtaining these they returned, got hold of military uniforms and all five set out for Louw's farm with eight horses, hired ostensibly by a 'British Officer'. The two Irishmen wore regular soldiers' uniforms, while Louis, who had white ancestry, posed as a Spanish sea-captain, in a blue coat with red and gold cuffs and epaulettes, wearing a sword by his side and a cocked hat with an ostrich feather. Abraham and Adonis passed as his batmen.

When they arrived at Pieter Louw's farm he was away, but his wife was completely taken in, and felt very honoured by the visit, offering dinner and lodgings for the night. Abraham and Adonis checked that the slaves hadn't had a change of heart (they had not), and everything seemed to be going according to plan.

That night, Hooper and Kelly got cold feet. They tiptoed into Louis's bedroom, quietly removed the blue jacket, sword and hat, slipped out of the window and hot-footed it to Saldanha Bay, where they were hoping to board a ship and flee.

Louis awoke and saw what had happened, but resolved to stick to the plan. Ten slaves and one Khoikhoi farmhand joined him. They seized the wagon and horses and set off to the neighbouring farm of Willem Basson. Basson was also away and Louis announced that he had been sent by the Government to free the slaves and take the farmers to Cape Town. Basson's wife managed to get away, but they tied up his son and took all the guns and ammunition, as well as the wagon and horses and set off to the next farm.

The procedure was repeated and within the following three days, thirty-four farms had been visited in the Zwartland, Koeberg and Tygerberg areas. Farmers were tied up in the wagons and the mob grew. However, many farm slaves refused to join them and, by the time they decided to march on Cape Town, they numbered only 326 men.

On the evening of 27 October a farmer carried the news to the Governor of the Cape, who immediately sent a large contingent of cavalry and infantry to intercept the band. The slaves put up no resistance and were all captured without a shot being fired. The farmers in the wagons were released and the slaves taken to Cape Town to stand trial. When the authorities realised that most of the slaves had been deceived, only fifty-one were tried for insurrection. Meanwhile Hooper and Kelly, the two main ringleaders, failed to find a ship, were hunted down and brought back to the Castle.

Something needs to be said here about British law and justice at that time. There were no less than 146 crimes that were punishable by death, including murder, rape and theft! Those found guilty of more serious crimes, such as treason and insurrection, were partly hanged, drawn whilst still alive, then cut into quarters and their remains were tied up at the North, South, East and West entrances to the town, to serve as a deterrent to others. Torture and public floggings of 100 lashes were commonplace until the early 19th century.

In December 1808 the High Court sentenced sixteen of the slaves to be hanged in public and their bodies were to be chained and publicly exhibited at different places to serve as a warning to others. The rest of the slaves were to be forced to attend the proceedings. Eventually, only Hooper, Louis, Abraham and two others were hanged and exhibited, and so ended the first slave revolt at the Cape.

The second revolt, in 1824, was a short but very bloody affair, culminating in the culprits' heads being cut off and fixed upon poles planted along the roads for all to witness – a grim way indeed to treat people during an equally grim period of history.

Deserted towns – Marabastad

T he Voortrekkers, under the leadership of the very quarrelsome
Stephanus Schoeman, left Ohrigstad and headed northwards to
the Soutpansberg. They established a new frontier town,
Zoutpansdorp, which would be eventually renamed Schoemansdal. But
petty infighting and squabbling was so rife that they even named a range
of mountains after the discord – the Strydpoortberge.

The dissention was so great that Field Cornet Jan Botha decided to
halt the trek, settle down in one place and patch up the quarrels. They
settled on the banks of the Sand River, some 20 km north-east of present-
day Pietersburg, and here he built a dam and a small fort he called Fort
Klipdam. Some years later, when the BaVenda drove the settlers out of
Schoemansdal in the Soutpansberg, the Klipdam settlement was revived.
A new fort was built on the same site, although this time it was a rather
ornate structure on the lines of a stylish medieval castle, with
battlements and crenellations.

This fort was an administrative outpost of the Transvaal Republic in
the 1880s and there lived Oscar Dahl, a short, stocky, powerful man,
born in Denmark. He had been a sailor, lured to South Africa by the
diamonds of Kimberley, and had later wandered up to open a trading
station in the Spelonken, in the Lydenburg district. He had fought with
the Boers in the First Sekhukhune War and had been appointed Native
Commissioner as a reward. After the annexation of the Transvaal in
1877, he fought in the Second Sekhukhune War with the British and they

had made him District Commissioner for the Northern Transvaal. With the restoration of the Republic after Majuba, he was left at his post, as he was both a popular and an efficient civil servant.

Oscar Dahl's wife Sannie was the half-sister of the famous Dina Fourie, the heroine of the tragic Sofala Trek, in which Dina's father, husband and children all had perished (see *The Story of Dina Chambers*). Part of Sannie's dowry were the two small 'Grietjie' cannons that had been the cause of the dreadful journey. These cannons, originally taken to Schoemansdal by Commandant Stephanus Schoeman, were handed over to João Albassini, known to the local people as 'Jowawa', when Schoemansdal was abandoned. Later they were given to a William Fitzgerald, who farmed on the Luvuvhu River, and he, in turn, gave them to Sannie, who presented them to her husband. Oscar mounted them on the twin turrets of his castle at Klipdam. When the Anglo-Boer War broke out, they were fitted with wheels taken from commandeered cocopans from the Eersteling Gold Mine, and brought into active service. Nowadays, this historic and much-travelled pair of cannons can be found in the Transvaal Museum in Pretoria.

Dahl, Officer of the Northern Transvaal frontier, was also the general civil service factotum, and among his general duties was that of marriage officer, in which regard an amusing story is told. One day, a shy young couple came to be married. Dahl completed the necessary formalities and then requested his fee. The cheeky young settler, referring to the time that Oscar had been a trader, said 'Put it down on the account.' Dahl flew into a rage, kicked the young man out, locked the door and shouted, 'I'll keep the bride – on deposit!'

Some time later, Sannie Dahl arrived back from a visit, saw the obviously distressed young man sitting in the garden and enquired as to the problem. The young man explained his predicament. She then sneaked into the house, took a pound note from her husband's best trousers, gave it to the young man and he redeemed his beloved!

Eventually, the Northern Soutpansberg settlers were forced out by Makhato, the Lion of the North and Chief of the BaVenda, and they all trekked away and settled south of Fort Klipdam in an area known as

Marabastad. It was never a successful settlement and, had it not been for the fact that Edward Button discovered gold on the farm Eersteling in 1871, it would have been abandoned years earlier. But the gold rush prolonged its life. At its peak it consisted of two marquee tents for Government officials, a boarding house, an interdenominational tin shanty church, four stores and a few shacks, along with five fine pubs, the best of these being 'The Blue Post' owned by L Page-Lee.

One of the Government tents doubled as the local gaol and was equipped with a set of stocks. Through some misunderstanding over a horse and spider, Bob Jameson, brother of the famous Leander Starr Jameson, was sentenced to three months in this gaol. Dr Bencome was horrified and warned Rabe, the Mining Commissioner, that Bob was a certified alcoholic and, if suddenly deprived of liquor, would certainly cause trouble. Rabe was impressed and ordered that Bob be allowed three drinks a day. So for three months a warder escorted Bob Jameson three times a day down to 'The Blue Post'. The last drink in the evening usually saw them swaying, arm in arm and singing, back to the tent. After this period in gaol, Bob Jameson walked off in the direction of Lourenco Marques, never to be seen in Marabastad again. Such was life in these frontier towns, full of interesting characters, many with a story to tell.

Marabastad, like many other frontier towns, was destined to vanish. The end of the gold rush removed its reason to exist and in November 1881 the new Volksraad decided to establish a town in the centre of the Northern Transvaal. A farm was purchased in a place known to the local people as Pholokwane ('the Protected Place') and this is the present-day Pietersburg. The local magistrate moved there in 1886 and Marabastad faded into history.

Willem Prinsloo – the reluctant farm seller

Many stories can be told of people who came to the diamond and goldfields and never made a cent. It seems that the first people there almost all died poor. To quote the words of an early Kimberley pioneer, Henry David Kisch, 'There is a curse on us very early comers', he said. 'I was on the diamond fields before Cecil John Rhodes was even thought of – before there was even a Kimberley. None of us who were there has a penny. Perhaps it doesn't matter, but it's timing – if you came too early you got nothing.'

An exception to this rule was a man named Willem Prinsloo, a fascinating character with an incredible life story. Prinsloo was a typical old Boer – white beard, felt hat and well-worn clothes. He had trekked to the Transvaal and settled on a property on the West Rand, called Modderfontein, where he farmed. Then came the prospectors and old Willem said that he wanted nothing to do with them, he wished to be left alone.

One day a man came to see Prinsloo. His name was J P Taylor of the mining house, Hermann Eckstein & Company. Asked what he wanted, Taylor replied that he was just returning from a hunt. 'You lie, Englishman', Prinsloo said, 'you are looking for gold'. He then refused to talk any further. Taylor decided that the only way to get to Prinsloo was through his wife and one evening, at milking time, he walked into the dairy and asked, 'What's that?'

'It's milk', replied Mrs Prinsloo.

'That's not milk – from how many cows did it come?'

'Six', replied Mrs Prinsloo.

'My poor woman, I have a cow in Johannesburg that will give you more than your six put together.' He then casually added that if he ever bought the farm, Mrs Prinsloo could have the cow and, if it did not fill that bucket twice a day, there would be no deal!

Late into the night Taylor could hear the old people discussing this wonder cow – whether she would have many calves and so on. The next morning Prinsloo said, 'Taylor, my wife gave me no rest about this cow. What do you offer for Modderfontein?'

'£30 000 cash and £40 000 in shares in the new gold Mining Company to be formed', Taylor replied.

Prinsloo left to speak to his wife. After the reassurance that the cow would fill the bucket twice a day, the deal was accepted and the cow delivered.

A few days later Taylor received a letter:

'Come to Pretoria on the 30th to accept transfer. The cow fills the bucket twice a day.

With compliments,

Willem Prinsloo.'

So the Modderfontein Gold Mining Company, forerunner of the New Modder, the Modder East and the Modder Deep was formed and floated with £200 000 capital and a working capital of £40 000. Willem received his shares, which he sold for £70 000, and moved to another district where he bought the farm Kaalfontein. It wasn't long, however, before those damned prospectors were at him again, this time for diamonds.

He allowed himself to be persuaded to sell for more than £100 000 cash and then moved to where he was sure they would not bother him again – about 30 km east of Pretoria, where he bought a sheep farm. It was with a certain satisfaction that he learnt that the Kaalfontein deposit had not been payable and that the buyers had lost their money. However, the money they had paid him had been safely put away.

Soon after the Second Anglo-Boer War, Willem Prinsloo saw the unmistakable signs of doom. There were men with picks, shovels and

93

sieves prowling around his fences. One day, a carpenter and builder came to see him. His name was Thomas Cullinan, and very tactfully he talked the old Boer into selling. 'Very well', said Prinsloo angrily, 'you can buy half the farm for £80 000. But you are not allowed to prospect on my half ever!'

With a face like thunder, Willem Prinsloo sold half his farm and the Premier Diamond Mine was floated. It became the greatest single man-made hole in existence – greater in area than the Kimberley hole. This was dug along his fence and yielded the biggest diamond in the history of the world, weighing over 3 000 carats. Willem Prinsloo, true to his word, sat tight on his half and there he died, as he had said he would.

If you ever drive out of Pretoria along the Witbank Highway, you will see the Willem Prinsloo Agricultural Museum on your left-hand side, a great reminder of a wonderful story.

Sekhukhune's Treasure

There are still people around who remember the name of Ikey Sonneberg, that colourful character from the early days of Kimberley and Pilgrim's Rest. But of all the stories related about him, none was as fascinating as Ikey's search for the treasure of Sekhukhune.

Sonneberg was not the first white man to hear the story about this treasure in the northern Transvaal and Sekhukhune's method of levying tribute from his subjects. It dated back to the 1870s when the original 'New Rush' was developing into the city of Kimberley. Thousands of black people from every part of South Africa found work on the diamond fields and Sekhukhune's Pedi people provided a substantial portion of that labour.

Before white men entered Griqualand West, Sekhukhune did not know of man's greed for diamonds, but once he did he resolved to profit from them. It was well known that no Pedi man was allowed to seek work on the diggings unless he brought back a diamond or a gold pound. The Chief knew that his men, eager to acquire the wherewithal to buy rifles, would not fail him. Nor did they.

In the late 1870s it became known that Sekhukhune possessed 'two blesbok skins of sovereigns and a gallon pot filled with diamonds'. Even if we discount the claim that the diamonds varied in size from pigeon's eggs upward, there is no doubt that the Chief had accumulated fantastic wealth. However, only he himself and a few handpicked indunas knew where the wealth was kept. At Pilgrim's Rest, it was the ambition of every digger – South African, Englishman, Scot, Australian and American – to find this treasure. They all tried to wheedle the secret from the wily old Chief.

The only man vaguely successful was a storekeeper named Dick Silk, who was told by Sekhukhune that one day perhaps he would be prepared to sell the gallon pot of diamonds. Silk told Ikey Sonneberg that he would need at least 1 000 gold sovereigns and Ikey raised the money. Together they went to Sekhukhune's kraal, high up in the mountains north-west of Lydenburg, where there was a natural fortress amongst the kloofs. They were led up a narrow footpath, past cattle kraals and huts, until they reached a flat space of ground that had been stamped hard. Here they were told to sit down.

After a suitable wait, Sekhukhune emerged. He proved to be a little man, with a shrewd look and very cautious in speech. The Chief eventually agreed to let them see the diamonds. 'Many of them were 30 to 40 carats in size', said Sonneberg, and the sight took his breath away. Ikey laid out the envelopes containing the 1 000 gold sovereigns, but their hearts sank when the Chief said, 'Yes, this is genuine gold, but I have no use for gold. I would rather keep the diamonds. The Boers are troubling me and I believe that they will soon wipe me out. If you can bring me a cannon, not only will I let you have the diamonds, but I will send a thousand labourers to your diamond fields to find more stones for you!'

The argument that gold could buy anything, even a cannon, did not impress the Chief and, with heavy hearts, they bade him goodbye and left.

As you may know, Sir Garnet Wolseley later defeated Sekhukhune and his lands were overrun. The treasure, according to one source, was hidden under Sekhukhune's hut. The British soldiers dug up the floor, but found nothing. Another story was that it was hidden in one of the innumerable caves nearby. During the 1880s, various syndicates were formed to hunt for Sekhukhune's millions, without success.

Sekhukhune's practice of demanding payment from his labourers was continued by Chief Magoto, who lived deep in the recesses of the

Soutpansberg. During 1908 both the Transvaal Treasury and the Department of Mines officially confirmed the existence of his huge hoard. It is believed that upon his death, the treasure passed to the famous Rain Queen, Modjadji of the BaLobedu or Lovedu. During the Boer War, Modjadji foresaw trouble and sent the diamonds down to the low country, to a place of greater safety. She chose a country of deadly malaria to which the messengers themselves fell victim.

It is said that when they felt the sickness coming, they hid the treasure near the wayside. And there it remains, its location unknown, to this very day.

The quiet recluse

In the pleasant Surrey town of Red Hill, just outside of London, a discrete and quiet old man named Maurice Marcus lived in retirement. He had been a part of this small community for so long that most had forgotten his arrival almost half a century before. Very little was ever known about him, other than his polite greetings when taking a stroll down the avenue, or playing his daily game of golf. His splendid residence was named Hightrees, situated behind a tall stone wall, well screened from passers-by. The very size of the house indicated that its owner was a man of substance, yet he led an exceedingly quiet and retiring life, preferring to do most of his negotiations through his lawyer, Mr Brown, or his housekeeper, Mrs McIntosh. Once in a while Mr Marcus would go to London to visit his nieces and an old cousin, but the visits were never reciprocated, and of his immediate family nothing was known. All that was known was that in his younger days, he had been in South Africa.

After the end of World War I he gave up his golf and it was noticed that on his daily walk down the avenue, his gait had become a little unsteady. On 14 September 1924, at the age of eighty-one, and almost unknown to his neighbours, Maurice Marcus slipped the mortal bonds of this earth.

After the usual valuations and will registration at Somerset House, the state inventory was made public. The figures were of such a scale that people could not associate them with the old man, who had lived in obscurity among them for so long. Maurice Marcus had a net worth of £3 145 751. The death duties alone came to more than £1 300 000. Then came the bequests:

£10 000 each to the Reigate and Red Hill hospitals
£5 000 to Guy's Hospital
£1 000 to a London hospital
£2 000 to the Jewish Board of Guardians; and
£1 000 each to his lawyer, his engineer and his housekeeper.
The rest went to his relations:
£50 000 to his sister Isabella Marcus
£100 000 to each of his nieces, Priscilla Joseph and Cecile Proctor and
£50 000 each to Edward Marcus and Gwendolyn Thornton.
The residue was to be split amongst his five nieces.

The heirs were thunderstruck. They had known he had a bit of money, but they had not imagined this kind of wealth. Where did all the money come from? They decided to go to South Africa and try to find out. They spoke to many ageing pioneers and finally managed to piece together the story of this most unusual man.

Maurice Marcus came to South Africa in 1862 to seek his fortune. He had just turned twenty when he arrived in Grahamstown and found a job, at £15 per month, with Mr Gowie, a grocer. He wrote to his uncle, John Marcus, who lived in the frontier town of Burgersdorp asking whether he could offer anything better. John Marcus was a friend of J B Robinson, then a trader at Bethulie in the southern Free State, as yet unconnected with any mining operations. He had the finest trading store in all the platteland and traded largely with the Boers. In 1863 he hired Maurice as a bookkeeper. Maurice was a pleasant, honest young man and he worked hard for five years at Bethulie. Just prior to the discovery of diamonds, J B Robinson made Maurice his partner.

Robinson set off to buy farms in the area where diamonds had been discovered and sent back instructions to Maurice: 'Follow me, bring all the natives you can find, buy all the oxen, cattle and wagons you can and come quickly.' Maurice carried out his instructions to the letter. He found twelve ox-wagons, bought 500 head of cattle and, with all the labour he could muster, he set off for the 'New Rush' area.

In those days the tribal people knew nothing about the value of diamonds, big or small, and would trade them for oxen. J B and Maurice were among the few who had cattle to trade and, besides the oxen, Maurice had also managed to bring 170 milk cows. The milk was as precious as the diamonds themselves.

Very soon J B Robinson sent Maurice to England with the first parcel of diamonds ever exported from South Africa, while Robinson carried on buying up more stones. 'We saw men making £5 000 per day for weeks on end', it was recorded, and on one occasion, J B did one million pounds worth of business in just two days. For a time six to ten carats per 100 loads was considered fair!

The two men stayed together for several years at Kimberley. Then in the 1880s, with the discovery of gold, J B Robinson proceeded to the Witwatersrand to set up his gold mining companies, the Robinson Deep mine and Randfontein Estates, which are still well known to this day.

Maurice preferred to supervise the London end of the business, and very soon they separated by mutual consent. 'I visited him again in 1888', said Robinson. 'He was already living at Hightrees, but I found him quiet and very retiring.'

Maurice Marcus never married and for the rest of his life he remained in Red Hill, Surrey, quietly drawing income from his millions and completely forgotten in the town and country where he had originally made his fortune – Kimberley, South Africa.

Tembe – the dry-land steamer

I believe that within the gene pool of the people of our magnificent country, lie strains of perseverance and tenacity of unbelievable proportions. The story that follows will, I hope, illustrate my point.

John Thorburn, born in England, went across to America at an early age. There he was, among other things, a planter and slave trader and he survived the Civil War. The discovery of diamonds attracted him to South Africa and, after a spell of working both the wet and dry diggings, he left the fields and became a storekeeper on the banks of the Lekoa or Vaal River. Business was good until the floods came and swept the lot downstream.

Undaunted, borrowing clothes from neighbours, he started again. Then he hit on the idea of a better way of making money. He wanted to ship goods down the Vaal to Kimberley. After securing the promise of supplies from neighbouring farmers and the necessary permissions from landowners, he wrote to Edwards and Symes in England to order a steam launch.

With a steel hull 11 m in length, a beam of 2,5 m, drawing 55 cms of water and powered by a 4 kW engine driving twin screws, the steam launch was soon under construction. In the meantime, Thorburn busied himself, for three years, clearing obstacles and even islands out of the way. He also constructed a large barge that could hold 300 tons, suitable for shipping coal from Vereeniging to Kimberley.

In 1883 the steamer was shipped to Cape Town and railed to the Beaufort West railhead, from where it was packed on ox-wagons and

101

carted in pieces up to the river. The experiment had thus far cost him over £4 000. But alas, once the launch, which was christened the *Tembe,* was assembled and put in the river, it was found that it drew too much water. So began a series of marches with the largest parcel ever conveyed across the South African veld. With local assistance the boat was lifted out of the water and lashed onto two wagons chained end to end and drawn by a quadruple span of oxen. Thus the trip to Potchefstroom began. Upon arrival Thorburn heard that Colonel Charles Warren was leading the British troops up to Bechuanaland to annex it. The *Tembe* was taken out of the water, again lashed onto wagons and trekked downstream to Warrenton, a distance of some 350 km. Upon arrival there was another surprise – Colonel Warren had already crossed the Vaal. Undaunted, Thorburn turned around and trekked back to the highveld, where he cleaned and repainted the boat. Now convinced that the Vaal River was not navigable, he invited tenders to take the *Tembe* to Delagoa Bay. The prices were too high and nobody would guarantee delivery, so he decided to do it himself.

The Landdrost of Potchefstroom, one John Kock, was very sceptical about this, but John Thorburn said to him, 'I will start with her on two wagons, and as long as the wheels go round, I will continue. When the wheels stop going round, I will see what the cause is and fix it until they go around again.' Kock patted him on the shoulder and said, 'I think you will reach the coast after all!'

In May 1884 this strange caravan, with John Thorburn Snr, John Jnr, George Grey and Bill Davies, along with many labourers, left Potchefstroom on the journey eastwards and its arrival in the small towns along the route caused quite a stir. The journey took fourteen months, first across the Witwatersrand – there was no Johannesburg then – then turning eastwards. At Bronkhorstspruit, at the drift where Colonel Anstruther and the 94th Regiment of Foot had been ambushed some four years earlier, a bad veld fire nearly stopped them, but they pushed on. At one stage the road was so bad that they could manage only two kilometres in four days!

On entering the eastern Transvaal, the road became unbelievably bad and they had to lay stone pathways – 'Ready… Go!' – and the whip would crack – 'Keep it in the middle!' Away went the front wheel, burying itself deep into the mud, leaving the wagon and its cargo half-suspended in mid-air. Out would come the ropes and the screw jacks and, eventually, after a couple of hours' hard work, the journey would continue. Somewhere near the headwaters of the Vaal River, some 2 000 metres above sea-level, progress was made by laying six-metre planks in front of the wheels and using crowbars to lever the wagons forward. John and his son went ahead to find a way through Buffels Heights and eventually, somewhere in Swaziland, the wagons lurched badly and overturned, smashing the *Tembe's* cabin and fittings into matchwood. Luckily nobody was killed, but the one side of the *Tembe* was knocked flat, six steel plates ripped open, the rivets were drawn and the iron bulkhead doubled up.

Faced with the situation of his launch lying 2 000 metres up in the Swaziland mountains, and all his savings invested in the wreck, Thorburn remained optimistic. Somehow he managed to repair the damage and pressed on. Eventually, leaving the craft with some traders, he walked on to Mozambique. But the trip was not over. A road had to be built to get the ship from the mountains to the coast and, to cap it all, he had to return to Potchefstroom as his youngest son had died. It was only in 1886 that he returned to his beloved steamer, this time bringing his wife with him. Eventually the boat was safely launched on the Thembe River, its boilers fired up, and away downstream sailed the *Tembe*. Not many days later, the startled Portuguese saw her heave to at the mouth of the Rio Espirito Santo. So ended the strange and fascinating boat trip of over 2 000 km on dry land.

John Thorburn made another attempt at a shipping enterprise. He led the team that brought the first steamer from the coast to Lake Tanganyika, but this also yielded him no profit, and so he returned to the Transvaal. His daughter married the well-known aviation pioneer, Allister M Miller, and another of his family, A R Thorburn, later became the mayor of Johannesburg.

Certainly, the genes of guts and determination I spoke of earlier must still be around to this day.

Of doctors and discoveries – Dr Atherstone

I t is rare indeed that fate allows a person more than once to occupy centre stage in the theatre of fame and fortune. But this did happen to Dr William Guybon Atherstone, celebrated surgeon, botanist, geologist, musician, artist and statesman. The first event made him a household name in his own country and the second, twenty years later, made him world-famous.

He was two years old when he arrived with his father, Dr John Atherstone, in South Africa in 1820. Later in life, he took up residence in Grahamstown where he attended Stephenson's Grammar School, at the famous Yellow House. After a spell at Uitenhage, he returned to Grahamstown in 1831 where he was apprenticed to his father, in order to qualify for the medical profession.

A few years later, at the age of sixteen, he was appointed Staff Medical Officer to the Governor, Sir Benjamin D'Urban, during the Sixth Frontier War. By the age of eighteen he was a fully qualified medical practitioner!

One incident that left a deep impression upon the young man was his interview with the famous Voortrekker leader, Piet Retief. News reached Dr John Atherstone that his friend Retief was going to lead one of the Treks. Much perturbed, he and William rode over to Mooimeisies-fontein, to persuade Retief to abandon his plan and stay. However, Retief was adamant and, bidding his friends a sorrowful farewell, he chose his path of destiny – one that ended on a lonely hill at Umgungundlovu in February 1838. One cannot help but wonder what the course of South African history would have been, had the persuasion of Atherstone senior been successful.

The day, Wednesday, 16 June 1847, was a memorable one in the annals of South African surgery, for it was on this day that Dr William Guybon Atherstone performed the first operation in this country using anaesthetics. Before the advent of anaesthetics, an operation was a nightmarish horror of incredible shock and excruciating agony for the patient concerned, so it is fitting that both Dr Atherstone and his patient, one Frederick Carlisle, should be remembered. *The Grahamstown Journal* published an article about the operation ten days later.

Mr Carlisle, Deputy-Sheriff of the Albany district, had all but lost the use of his leg and gangrene was starting to set in. He said the pain was so unbearable that he would gladly have his leg amputated if the pain would stop. After several experiments using different kinds of apparatus, with and without valves, Dr Atherstone succeeded in producing the required degree of insensibility, by means of a simple hubble-bubble container from a hookah pipe.

The patient, convinced of the powerful effects of ether, consented to have the leg removed, but stipulated that the operation could not start until he gave the word. After ten to twelve inhalations of the ether, he reached down and pinched himself, then continued to inhale a short while longer, pinched himself again and said 'I'm drunk enough now – you may begin!' The tourniquet was immediately tightened and at the same moment the first incision was made. The patient did not feel or show any signs of discomfort, still mechanically opening and closing his nostrils with his own hand. So perfect was the insensibility that the assistants let go of the patient altogether. For the rest of the operation, Carlisle lay motionless on the bed. Once the leg was removed and the nerves and blood-vessels taken care of, the bottle was removed and the patient, still holding his nose, became talkative and even humorous as he gradually recovered from the stupefying effects.

He had inhaled ether for about four minutes. He then asked, 'Why have you removed the bottle of vapour?'

Atherstone replied, 'Because the operation is over, your leg has been off for some time now.'

'Don't talk nonsense to me Doctor', said Carlisle, 'I'm a reasonable man, just tell me why you have removed the bottle.'

'You don't require it any longer, your leg is off!'

'Impossible, I don't believe it, let me see for myself.' Upon seeing the stump, he said, 'God be praised, this is the greatest discovery ever made. I have been totally unconscious of everything – the sound of the saw still rings in my ears, as if in a dream from which you awoke me, but I never felt any pain ever!'

So the first trauma-free operation was recorded in *The Grahamstown Journal,* and preserved for posterity. But as far as Dr William Atherstone was concerned, fate had a much more far-reaching event in store, one that would make him renowned in the world.

Some twenty years later Dr Atherstone, who in the meantime had become quite well known as a geologist, received a strange parcel in the post. He carelessly tore it open and read the covering letter.

Colesberg
March 12
1867

My dear Sir,
I enclose a stone which has been handed to me by one John O'Reilly, as having been picked up on a farm in the Hope Town district, and as he thinks it is of some value, I send the same to you to examine, after which you must please return it to me.

Yours very sincerely,
Mr Lorenzo Boyes
Acting Civil Commissioner
Colesberg.

Atherstone was greatly excited and rushed off to the local jeweller, Mr Galpin. Galpin tested the stone for hardness and agreed that it was a diamond. On the way home, the excited Atherstone saw Professor Peter MacOwen and showed him the stone. MacOwen suggested that in order to make absolutely certain, they should test the stone's specific gravity. Off they went to the house of the Catholic Bishop, the Right Reverend James Richards, and there in the Bishop's study, with a hair pulled from Atherstone's head and fastened with a small bit of wax on the stone, they completed the specific gravity test. The results were positive. The Bishop grabbed the diamond, strode over to the window pane and scratched his initials on the glass. This pane is still in the Roman Catholic Presbytery in Grahamstown, with the inscription 'Initials of the Rt Rev James David Richards – cut with the first diamond discovered in South Africa, 1867'.

Sir Percy Douglas, the Lieutenant Governor of the Eastern Cape, had just returned to Grahamstown and a state dinner had been organized for that night. Atherstone thought this a fine opportunity to make his discovery known, and he whispered to a friend, Advocate Henry Blaine, that during the toasts he was going to stand up and make his announcement. Blaine was horrified. 'For heaven's sake, Doctor, don't do it – remember the Sand River Gold.' He was referring to a previous statement Atherstone had made at a similar dinner, claiming that gold had been discovered in the Orange Free State. The 'discovery' had proved to be fraudulent and Henry Blaine, knowing the doctor's optimistic nature, wished to save him from further embarrassment, but to no avail. Amid a great hush, the doctor rose to his feet and made the announcement that was to have such far-reaching effects on the economy of our country, and continues to do so to this very day.

Dr Atherstone wrote to Boyes congratulating him and informing that the stone was a 21,25 carat diamond worth £500. The stone was sent to Cape Town, acquired by the Governor, Sir Philip Wodehouse and sent to the Crown jewellers Hurst & Boskell in London, who confirmed the analysis. It was then proudly sent on to the Paris Exhibition for display.

Not much happened after that, as people were very sceptical. One said that the place in which it was discovered was salted with diamonds from Brazil. Another put forward the interesting theory that ostriches must have deposited the diamonds there. But the optimistic Atherstone would not be discouraged.

Fortunately, an even more bizarre event then took place. We have learnt how Honest John O'Reilly handed the first diamond to Mr Boyes of Colesberg. Boyes gave Van Niekerk, the farmer, on whose land he had picked it up, his half-share, £250, and this then got the old farmer thinking. If just one of these 'worthless' stones was worth £500, he must try to find more of them.

He remembered that a Bushman whom he knew had a similar, but larger stone, which he carried in a dirty old skin bag around his neck. Van Niekerk set off to find the Bushman, but failed, as he had wandered off into the wilds. Van Niekerk left a message for the man to contact him when he returned.

One morning Van Niekerk awoke to find the Bushman patiently waiting for him on his veranda. He had the bag around his neck. To the Bushman's absolute amazement, the farmer gave him 500 sheep, 10 oxen and a horse for the stone. Van Niekerk then set out for Hopetown, where the stone was examined and declared to be an 83,5 carat white diamond. Van Niekerk sold it to Lilienfeld Brothers for £11 200 and returned home a rich man.

The stone was sent to England and was subsequently purchased by Lady Dudley for £2 500. This is how the famous 'Star of South Africa' came into existence.

In this way the South African diamond rush began, with incalculable results for our country and, although many far bigger stones were subsequently found, such as the Cullinan Diamond weighing 3 025 carats, not one has ever had such far-reaching effects as that small 21,25 carat stone which so excited Dr William Atherstone on that day in 1867.

John Hepke and the silver mine

D uring the Anglo-Boer War of 1899–1902, a little-known skirmish took place in the Broederstroom area, at a place called Kalkheuvel, lying on the left hand side of the Broederstroom road, opposite the Alpha Training Centre in Gauteng.

During this brief engagement the British column was commanded by General French and the Boers of the Wolmaransstad Commando by Commandant Du Toit. A Boer marksman wounded a British Officer, John Hepke. As was often the case during that war when the wound was not life-threatening, the bullet remained inside. He was bandaged up and left to recover, as the facilities of the field hospitals were very rudimentary. John Hepke survived the war and went back to Britain. Some time later, he fell ill and after many tests he was diagnosed as having lead poisoning. They removed the bullet, which they then had assayed to confirm the correct diagnosis of the disease. They gave him the bullet as a memento along with the assay report. He was amazed to learn in the report that the bullet had an extremely high silver content. Those of you who have a knowledge of geology and mining will know that lead and silver usually occur together in deposits.

This information perplexed Hepke and after a while he decided to return to South Africa, where he retraced his steps in the foothills of the Magaliesburg to Kalkheuvel, where he had been wounded. An old Afrikaner farmer, who owned the property, accompanied him. When they reached the battle site, Hepke was amazed not to find any spent cartridges lying around. He said to the Boer, 'I cannot believe this, as I was shot here and know how many shots were fired.' The old farmer replied, 'Don't be silly, we Boers were very poor and after you people had retired to Rietfontein West, we sent in the children to pick up the spent cartridges, which we would then reload.'

'Oh', said Hepke, 'and where did you obtain the lead?'

'From a small lead mine on an adjacent farm just south of here', replied the farmer. Hepke asked the farmer to take him to this little mine, which had been abandoned shortly after the war. John Hepke bought the farm on which this mine was situated, immigrated to South Africa and began working the little mine, which he named the Lonely Hand Silver Mine. He never made a fortune out of the mine, but worked it profitably for many years. His son, John Hepke junior, split up the farm some time later and sold off portions. In his sixties, he retired to Cape St Francis in the Eastern Cape. If you are in the area of Broederstroom, as you drive towards Hennops River into the foothills of the Magaliesburg, you will see, on your left hand side, the Silver Hills Gemstone. It stands as a memorial to a big man, with a story that should not be forgotten.

The Malmani goldfields

The huge rush in the late 1880s to the Witwatersrand, with all its clamour and hype, tended to divert attention from other gold discoveries of that period. They too each possess stories well worth relating.

Apolay Pillatt started one of these small rushes when, in August 1886, he claimed to have discovered gold on the farm Stinkhoutboom, situated close to the Malmani River in the Zeerust district of what is now the North West Province. The diggers on their way to the Witwatersrand promptly turned west to investigate the new finds. Prospectors such as Thomas Sephton and Michael Kelly found more traces of gold on adjoining farms and a gold rush began. It was quite violent in its suddenness. In a period of a few months the tiny settlement of Malmani boasted a string of mills to crush ore, and four hotels featuring, in addition to the usual diversions, sophisticated entertainments such as dancing girls! On 7 February 1887 the farm Zeekoevlei, belonging to Mr G Pretorius, was thrown open as a public goldfield to be taken up by prospectors and diggers – and the boom was on.

President Paul Kruger hated these places, with their drunkenness, bar brawls and men paying for the favours of the hotel dancing girls in gold dust. It went against the grain of the sternly Calvinistic beliefs of the rural Afrikaner. Nevertheless, he paid it a visit on his annual tour of the ZAR and was presented with the usual petition of grievances and desires.

By the middle of 1888, values were dropping as the gold-bearing seams were pinched out and started disappearing altogether. By October 1888 most hopes were wrecked and half the camp had packed up and left for the better prospects of the Witwatersrand. The hotels, the glamour and the girls were no more. Only the die-hard diggers and people resisting change were still wandering around the hushed place, like earth-bound ghosts. Malmani drew one last breath in 1895, when a supposed extension of the Witwatersrand reef was discovered, but this too pinched out and came to nothing, and another boom town died.

In 1895 it was surveyed, renamed Ottoshoop after the District Magistrate, Cornelius Otto, and turned into a little agricultural hamlet. Little has changed to this day. Its only claim to fame was that it became the meeting place for the troops from Pretoria and Mafikeng who, once they had joined up, marched on towards Johannesburg during what came to be called the Jameson Raid.

In 1899 a prominent firm in Johannesburg auctioned off a rare bowl made from the gold of the Malmani field. To my knowledge it went to a local collector. It must be one of the only pieces of memorabilia in existence from that hectic place, and very valuable indeed.

The 'towenaar' of Humansdorp

endrik Spoorbek, born at Dortmund in Germany, arrived at the
Cape in 1811 as a sailor and promptly 'jumped ship'. Four years
later, in 1815, we find him in Humansdorp. We know this
because 'Spoorbek se Erf' was registered as a quitrent farm and cost five
rixdollars per annum. Unfortunately, the farm is no longer visible as it
forms part of the dam on the Krom River.

Ou Spoorbek was a 'Towenaar', or magician, in the folklore of the
Afrikaners of the Eastern Cape. In 1901, a schoolteacher by the name of
J R van der Merwe, recorded many of the tales told about Spoorbek, and
fortunately these have been preserved.

Spoorbek was an untidy, woolly-haired, bearded, eccentric hermit
who rode a white horse and loved to teach people manners. In one story
he had stayed overnight at a farmhouse. As he left the following
morning, he heard the farmer's wife say to her husband, 'Look, the old
pig has forgotten his tobacco pouch.' Spoorbek returned later that day
and said to her, 'Look, the old pig has forgotten his tobacco pouch!' The
couple were deeply embarrassed.

On another occasion, as he was walking down one of Humansdorp's
dusty streets, a young couple passing by, said, 'Look, there goes the old
Towenaar.' Spoorbek froze, then turned and said, 'You two think that you
will marry – you never will.' It is not surprising therefore to learn that, as
the priest was reading the wedding service, the bride left the church by
one door and the groom by another. The service was never completed.

Spoorbek made a measly income by casting spells on the thatched roofs of homesteads. Many a tale is told of how the contents of the house would burn, but never the thatch, and his fame spread throughout the district.

One such recorded incident took place in the little hamlet of Alexandria, then called Kerkplaats, east of Port Elizabeth, during the Sixth Frontier War of 1834–35. The Xhosa attacked the settlement when Spoorbek happened to be there. Homesteads were plundered and burnt. Three hundred head of cattle and sheep were taken and the settlers retreated into the local schoolhouse for a last defensive stand. Across the road was the church and everywhere Xhosa warriors were running, shooting, shouting, looting and burning the town. The people in the schoolhouse fired and reloaded and fired again. The Xhosa set fire to the church's thatch roof and Spoorbek said, 'Be calm – the schoolhouse roof will not burn.' The Xhosa came with burning branches and flung them onto the roof. The settlers kept firing, the Xhosa were driven back and, miracle of miracles, the roof did not burn.

The church, which was built in 1830 by that well-known Voortrekker, Karel Landman, was razed to the ground and had to be rebuilt, but the schoolhouse remained standing.

Years later, in 1873, the schoolhouse roof was replaced with corrugated iron by Martinus Scheepers, an elder of the Church, and the townsfolk all gathered around for the now familiar test, but the thatch would not take the flame. The townspeople gathered the thatching and carried it away to their homes.

Such was the folkloric fame of this strange man. He was buried on his farm on 13 June 1845 and, although the farm was flooded, his grave stays above the water-level. I trust that the old schoolhouse and church are now monuments to his memory.

The strange Ohrigstad phenomena

I t is not very often that I record non-human stories, but the one I am going to describe is, I feel, well worth a mention. Quite some time ago, whilst visiting the Lydenburg district of Mpumalanga, ferreting out aspects of our country's magnificent peoples and their histories, I came upon the story of the strange phenomena.

My friends, Alistair and Marion Moirs, and I were travelling from Burgersfort towards Ohrigstad when suddenly Alistair pointed to a mountain range up ahead. It was a short range, but quite high. 'Have I ever told you the story of the farm up there?' he asked. When I said no, he stopped the car and proceeded to tell the most incredible story.

This saga started about thirty-five years ago when a local farmer in the area, Duppie Papenfus, bought the farm Nooitgedacht 487 KT. Straddling the top of the highest part of the mountain, it had never been farmed before. It was virgin bush. Duppie acquired a bulldozer at a local auction and proceeded to carve a road up the side of the mountain. At night he used to camp out in a small tent next to the Vyfenhoekspruit, originally called the Mamatali, which has its source at the top of the range. Some years later, when the farm was running and the homestead completed, the Moirs often were invited over for a Sunday braai. The scene was a very familiar one in our country, with the children playing and the adults chatting over a few cold beers. The children would always come to Duppie and ask for some bread. 'What for?' he asked one day. 'To feed the hungry snake in the river', was the reply. The adults just laughed and carried on their conversations and off the children would go, to return some time later.

One day Duppie's curiosity got the better of him and, after giving them the requested bread, he followed them at a distance. Down to the stream they went and then, keeping dead quiet, the eldest of the children put her index finger into the water and moved it up and down and side to side. Suddenly a head appeared out of the water, and Duppie stood dumbfounded as the children proceeded to feed an extremely large freshwater eel!

The Papenfus family was so amazed that they called in freshwater zoologists from a university and the following amazing facts emerged. These freshwater eels, upon reaching maturity, leave the peaceful ponds of that far-away mountain and travel down the Vyfenhoekspruit. They journey with the stream that flows down through Casper's Nek (named after Paul Kruger's father) into the Blyde River, and then into the Olifants. This eventually links up with the Limpopo and goes down all the way through Mozambique to reach the sea at Xai Xai! The eels then swim away from the Mozambique coastline, travelling eastwards until they finally reach Morondava Bay on the west coast of Madagascar. Here they mate and spawn. The total distance travelled is 1 870 kilometres.

The second half of the story is even more incredible. The young eels or elvers start the journey back to Mozambique and, by some still unexplained DNA memory bank cell, these elvers reach Xai Xai. Up the Limpopo they go, against the current all the time, up into the Olifants, then left into the Blyde and eventually the Vyfenhoekspruit and up the mountain – back to those self-same ponds from where their parents started the long journey many months before. This means that these eels, in their lifetime, complete a total of over 3 700 km, travelling half of that entire distance against the current.

I was ignorant enough to doubt the story until, some months later, I watched a BBC TV programme on the Scottish freshwater eels. These eels come down the Firth of Forth, go south around Britain and then head westwards – to spawn in Massachusetts Bay, off the east coast of the

116

United States, over 6 000 km away! And then the young start on the return journey.

That excellent reference book *Smith's Sea Fishes of Southern Africa* tells us that these eels in the Ohrigstad mountains could be any one of four varieties of South African freshwater eels and can attain 1,5 m in length and weigh up to 20 kg. They have been observed wriggling up wet vertical cliffs and scaling dam walls. On the Vyfenhoekspruit there is a 10 m waterfall. No wonder they make the uphill journey and climb whilst still young and very small.

What an astounding country we live in!

Steinacker's Horse

In the late 1890s, having got into trouble with the South West African Government, Ludwig Steinacker wandered down to Alfred County on the South Coast of Natal. There he managed the farm of Charles Reed, near Ivy Bay. He very soon sickened of the solitude and wandered off again to Marburg, Port Shepstone and became a barman in a local pub. Then the Anglo-Boer War broke out and Steinacker's moment in history had arrived.

Late in May 1900, a notice appeared in the British recruiting office in West Street, Durban:

WANTED
40 men for service in the Low Country.
Must be able to speak Dutch, a black language, and ride a horse.

All the volunteers were sent up to Pietermaritzburg and after the recruiting officer weeded out the unfit, five men were told to go to the Prince of Wales Hotel. There (surprise, surprise) they met the gamecock Steinacker, a very short, spare, bumptious man, who had convinced the British military authorities that he could raise a corps for a special task. They were treated to dinner and put on the overnight train to Durban, to be kitted out.

Then the adventures started. Without telling his men what their task was, Steinacker rode them up through Zululand, avoiding for security reasons all contact with human settlements. The first village they visited was Ubombo, way up in northern Zululand. All the way, Steinacker was recruiting frontiersmen – the toughest and hardest he could find. Very soon this corps was dubbed 'The Forty Thieves' and you will soon see why. They rode on up to Lomahasha on the northern border of Swaziland. There he revealed the plan, which was to blow up the bridge at Komatipoort on the Transvaal Republic's railway line to Mozambique. This was to prevent the retreating Boers from taking their big guns, stores and equipment out of the country.

One of the guards along the line was sympathetic to their cause and told Steinacker that he was too late – the Boers were already at Komatipoort. Steinacker and his men thereupon withdrew into the Swaziland bush and concocted an alternate plan to save face. On 17 June 1900 they blew up a culvert bridge near Malelane. When the pursuing British arrived they assumed that the Boers had blown up the culvert.

Steinacker once again retreated into Swaziland. On the strength of his 'success', he was promoted to the rank of Major and allowed to form a corps of 450 men, to be called Steinacker's Horse. They were given the task of creating as much of a nuisance as possible in Swaziland. They had their headquarters at Lomahasha and built a small fort with a heliograph station on Stegi Hill. In March 1901 they raided Manzini, or Bremersdorp as it was then called. Eight Boers were captured and the village was taken possession of. The whole place was ransacked. Buried under the floor of Gustav Swartz's store they found £600! Roving around Swaziland, they ransacked the store of one Stuart at Oshoek and found £3 500, also buried under the floor. Their actions resulted in notoriety and fame, depending upon which side you were on. Their cattle raiding expeditions into the Transvaal made them many enemies.

Steinacker's Horse consisted of 450 men and was one of the wildest corps ever known. It was, as the Boer General Viljoen said, 'A Corps formed of all the desperadoes and vagabonds scraped together in the North, including storekeepers, smugglers, spies and scoundrels of every description.'

There were certainly incredible characters present, including 'Devils

119

Own' McKenna, the brother of a British cabinet minister and Frank Lindh, who had deserted from both the British Brigade of Guards and the Royal Navy and had spent time in most of the gaols in South America. Others were Neville Edwards, George Bunting, Karshagen the German, Gaza Grey, Harry Wolhuter (later to become the famous game ranger), Little Evan Banger, one-time storekeeper from Merry Pebbles at Ry Koppies, Tommy Rathbone, Dave Buchanan and 400 others, along with a lanky Australian sergeant, with a cadaverous face and a mouth just made for drinking beer, who sported so many feathers in his hat that Steinacker called him 'a bloody fowl'. The corps was later expanded to 600 men and he was promoted to Lieutenant Colonel.

Steinacker's Horse was essentially a border guard and had posts at Ingwavuma, Isitigi, Lomahasha and pickets under Sergeant Robinson at Matibiskom and Komatipoort. North of Komatipoort they had outposts at Metsimetsi and Crocodile Bridge, one at Sabie Bridge, another on the Olifants River and one way up north at Shingwedzi, where old Corporal Perry and Sardelli the Greek were stationed. Some of these posts were supplied by the Selati Railway line, which is itself another interesting part of our past. Tom Boyd drove the steam engine, until he drank himself to death and then 'Clinkers' Churchill took over.

The Boers were now sick and tired of the havoc caused by this motley crew and General Tobias Smuts, with 150 men of the Ermelo Commando, set out on 23 July 1901 from Belskop. They rode throughout the night, encircled Bremersdorp and then, at 3 a.m. attacked from the south. However, during the night some Swazis had warned Steinacker and he had hotfooted it up to Lomahasha, leaving only thirty men in Bremersdorp. After a brief fight in which four of Steinacker's men were killed, they surrendered. The Boers spent the day celebrating, drinking and looting. They set fire to the town and all but the school and the gaol, which were built of stone, were razed to the ground. Then they rode away.

General Tobias Smuts was subsequently court-martialled by General Louis Botha for this incident and, at the end of the war, Bremersdorp was rebuilt and given the name Manzini, which it bears to this day.

Far off to the north, some 15 km north of Bushbuckridge, on the farm Orinoco, Steinacker's men built a fort they called Mpisanas with its garrison commanded by Captain 'Farmer' Francis. This garrison was particularly active in raiding cattle from the farms along the escarpment and General Ben Viljoen decided to liquidate them. Early on the morning of 6 August 1901 the commando crept towards the fort, jumped the trench and fired over the walls. The fort was taken and Captain Francis was killed. The Boers also captured fifty black cattle-guards and summarily shot them. However, they did not capture the cattle as these had been sent to Komatipoort some days before. This was the last action in which Steinacker's Horse took part. Steinacker received the Distinguished Service Medal and his corps was disbanded, in spite of his efforts to have it made into a permanent border guard.

Sardelli the Greek went off and sold the guns that he had accumulated during his service. Dougal McCorkindale went back to the Lebombo Mountains with many other frontiersmen and Steinacker himself went farming on 'London', just north of Bushbuckridge, where he tried to grow tobacco and cotton. The venture failed, he became bankrupt and was kicked off the farm. Jack Travers of Champagne Farm took him in as a handyman, where he earned enough for food and pocket money. Travers eventually asked him to leave. The request was ignored and Travers called the Bushbuckridge police, who came to arrest him and remove him to an internment camp. Steinacker told the police to wait whilst he gathered his belongings. After a few moments, he stumbled out of the door foaming at the mouth. In the heat and the dust he fell to the ground, dying, having swallowed strychnine. All he possessed was a revolver, a diary full of abuse and not a penny to his name.

The little gamecock was buried out there in the bush, with only a cairn of stones to mark his grave. Nobody was there to mourn his passing. But, I suppose, that is the way it usually was with frontiersmen. They lived hard and they died hard.

121

The Battle of Bronkhorstspruit

W hen Sir Theophilus Shepstone had Rider Haggard raise the British flag in Pretoria on 12 April 1877, thereby annexing the hopelessly insolvent Transvaal, it was perhaps inevitable that the burghers, would, at some stage, rebel against direct British rule. The Boers met on 8 December 1880 on the farm Paardekraal just outside Krugersdorp, elected the Triumvirate of Joubert, Kruger and Pretorius and went into revolt. The Governor, Sir Owen Lanyon, having for months played down the possibility of revolt, finally called for reinforcements. Colonel Colley was marching up from Natal and Colonel Anstruther, with the 94th Regiment, was instructed to leave Lydenburg post-haste and march on Pretoria. Anstruther dithered for fourteen days in Lydenburg, buying more transport wagons and stores and having the endless farewell parties that gallant officers were accustomed to.

On 5 December, with a 40-piece band leading the way, Anstruther's 'flying column', consisting of 9 officers and 254 other ranks, 3 women and 2 children and 16 large commissariat wagons, each drawn by a span of 18 oxen, left Lydenburg for Pretoria to the cheers of the people lining the street.

Because of the debacle of the Sekhukhune War, the British did not believe that the Boers would actually fight, and all warnings of the likelihood of an ambush, particularly in the hills to the east of Pretoria, were completely ignored. The 'flying column' averaged less than 15 km per day and, on 15 December, Colonel Anstruther received yet another warning from a mounted half-caste policeman about a possible Boer ambush. Again the warning was ignored – and no scouts were sent forward.

On the night of 19 December the officers and the men of the 94th bivouacked near Honey's Farm. The peach orchard was in full fruit. The troops helped themselves to the ripe peaches and stuffed their haversacks to the brim. The sergeants and officers tried to make good the situation by going to the farmhouse to apologise and pay the Boer vrou compensation. In the morning, with the band in full swing, and most of the men having unbuttoned their red serge tunics because of the hot December highveld sun and, having thrown their rifles onto the wagons, they were surprised when the band leading the column stopped playing. Out of the bush came a young Boer, with a white handkerchief tied to the muzzle of his rifle, bearing an envelope addressed to Colonel Anstruther, which he handed to Ralph Edgerton, the band's conductor. Anstruther, rode up to the front of the column, opened the envelope and read, 'We have declared the Transvaal a Republic and any movement of troops is disallowed. You are to turn around and go back to Lydenburg. For if you cross the Bronkhorstspruit, we consider it an act of war.'

Colonel Anstruther, still not believing that the Boers would fight, and not realising that Commandant Frans Joubert and his commando were lying only a short distance away with their rifles ready, said to the youngster, 'My orders are to go to Pretoria, and to Pretoria I will go.' Anstruther rather foolishly called for the opening of the ammunition boxes, whereupon Frans Joubert, considering this a hostile act, ordered his men to charge. They galloped to within 200 metres, dismounted and opened fire. The battle was over in less time than it takes to tell the story, and within fifteen minutes fifty-seven of the troops were dead and slightly over a hundred lay wounded in the dirt of that old road. The wounded Anstruther ordered his men to surrender.

The local Boer women on the surrounding farms nursed the British soldiers, but Anstruther, having received five wounds to his legs, died a few days later from shock, after amputation of one of his shattered legs.

All the British dead were buried in a mass grave alongside the road, and if you know where to go on the farm, which still belongs to the descendants of the same family, you can stand on that old dirt road leading to Lydenburg in the east and to Pretoria in the west.

Because the British soldiers were buried as they stood, the peaches they carried in their pockets and haversacks were buried with them. In 1901, during the second Anglo-Boer War, a column of British troops was marching eastwards from Pretoria when they came across 'two uncommonly fine orchards' of peach trees, growing out of the haversacks of those soldiers who lay buried beside the road. The old farmstead still has peachwood lintels over the windows and the family treasures letters and other relics of that skirmish.

The story of
Sarah Heckford

On 30 June 1839, in Dublin, Ireland, was born Sarah Maud Goff. From a landed gentry background, she inherited, on both sides of her family, a tradition of service. The army, the church and laws she learnt about from her father, and good works and community service from her mother. Along with a dose of puritanical intolerance and an independent turn of mind, this background in Victorian England assured her a position in society.

Her mother died when she was six years old and having contracted tuberculosis, she was doomed to be partially lame, with a slight hump on her right shoulder. She remained self-conscious about this and would never allow a photograph be taken from the left-hand side.

Sarah studied, becoming competent in music and painting and, at the age of twenty-two years found herself financially independent. At that time there were no women doctors in England and she began caring for the sick and poor. Sarah took her inspiration from Elizabeth Blackwell. Elizabeth was born in Bristol in 1821, emigrated to America in 1832, then studied medicine and was awarded a PhD in 1849. She obtained permission to study at St Bartholomew's Hospital in London. Both women met Florence Nightingale, who was at this time still living at home. What a tragedy it was that facilities in England for higher education were denied to women at that time!

In 1866 the great cholera epidemic, which had arrived from Egypt by ship, struck London. Extra nurses were desperately needed and Sarah volunteered. She met a doctor, Nathaniel Heckford from Calcutta, who was a mere twenty-two years of age, but had already won gold medals for medicine and surgery. On 28 January 1867, the twenty-six-year old Sarah married the twenty-three-year old Dr Heckford, much to the displeasure of her relations.

At this time there were no hospitals that would admit children under the age of two years, so Sarah took £4 000 of her debentures. In January 1868 they started the East London Hospital for children, in Butcher's Row. During this period Charles Dickens used to visit the hospital and they remained good friends until his death in 1870. Nathaniel, the love of Sarah's life, died in 1871 at the tender age of twenty-nine, and was buried in the Goff's cemetery plot in Woking, Surrey.

The British, represented by Sir Theophilus Shepstone, had annexed the Transvaal Republic in 1877, and the broken-hearted Sarah decided to make a new life for herself. She purchased 100 shares in the Transvaal Mining and Trading Association. Lame, widowed and in poor health, she set sail for South Africa. She arrived in December 1878 in Durban. Having bought a horse and, in the company of a transport rider, she rode into the Transvaal, westward to Rustenburg, where the business venture she had bought into was supposed to have been situated. She stayed at the local inn, only to discover that the whole thing was a hoax. The scheme did not exist. Her money was now running low and she realized that if she did not get a job with lodgings, she would be in desperate trouble.

The local clergyman arranged a post for her as a private tutor to the two Jennings daughters on the farm Nooitgedacht, in the Hekpoort valley. The Jennings' were quite a family themselves, being second-generation 1820 settlers who had trekked up to the Magaliesburg and started farming. This was a pleasant period for Sarah. In the winter months the family would trek up to the Northam region for the cattle to enjoy the winter grazing, returning to the farm with the onset of spring.

Sarah, however, was becoming restless and, having learned quite a lot about farming, she persuaded William Jennings to sell her a portion of the farm Groenfontein. It was during this period that she employed an Englishman named Edgerton, who was 'down on his uppers'. She then acquired a wagon and twelve 'salted' oxen, and decided to become an itinerant trader, a 'smous'. Male smouses were common then, but a woman smous – unheard of! She left Nooitgedacht and trekked to the markets of Pretoria, where she bought supplies of all sorts of commodities the farmers required. On the way home, she sold her goods along the valley. The northern part of the country was now being opened up, and she decided to ply her trade on the Great North Road. Northwards she travelled with Edgerton as her 'voorlooper', leading the oxen. She would trade her goods at settlements such as Marulaskop and the Nylstroom district, and then head back to Pretoria. On one of these expeditions she entered an agreement with Makopane (Makapan), trading very successfully in grain with the Chief until the outbreak of the so-called 'Gun War' in Basotuland caused a shortage of grain. She fell out with George Edgerton, her presumed lover, and he went off to the Basotu War never to be heard of again.

She soon realised that war between the Boers and their British rulers was imminent and moved onto the farm she had bought. The First Anglo-Boer War broke out in 1880. Anstruther was defeated at Bronkhorstspruit, Colley was defeated at Majuba, the British sued for peace and the Transvaal was returned to the Boers. This heralded the end for those farmers who had supported the British. Business in the Transvaal had collapsed. Banks were calling in their loans and many people were going bankrupt. She decided to head for Natal. On the way her oxen sickened and died, a Boer shot her beloved dog 'Prince' and at Harrismith, she gave up. She eventually made it to Durban where she sailed for England.

We know very little about Sarah's life between 1881 and 1887, other than the fact that she helped out in the East End Hospital. However, as happens with so many people who leave this country, the memory haunted her. She longed for the African sun and the bush and, in May 1888 she arrived in the boom-town of Johannesburg, where gold had been discovered only two years before. The bondholders had foreclosed on her farm and she set herself up as a sharebroker in Booysens. Her timing could not have been worse! March 1899 saw the mines hit pyrites and yields plummeted. The boom collapsed almost overnight and the biggest slump in the history of Johannesburg began.

Sarah weathered the storm, found a buyer for her farm, settled the bond and, with the little that was left, she decided to go transport-riding and farming. She bought a 'Burgher's right' farm out near Middelburg on the road to Mozambique, invested in two wagons with oxen and set about remaking her fortune by transport-riding on the Great North Road. It was here that she found the ideal farm, 'Tobias zyn Loop', and, when the railway came, she was bought out at a handsome profit. The business grew, especially now that she had the capital for trading. She moved to the northern Transvaal, loaded her wagons and travelled the 110 kilometres down the Klein Letaba area, where she supplied the miners at the Birthday Mine with their requirements. She bought the farm Ravenshill and worked out the first farm-schooling scheme in the Transvaal, launching the Transvaal Women's Educational Union in 1898.

In 1902, after the Second Anglo-Boer, she sailed for England, where she was treated as a celebrity. She caused a sensation by attacking Emily Hobhouse, declaring how very little the latter actually knew about the entire situation! She soon returned to the Transvaal and took lodgings on the corner of Du Toit and Schoeman Street, Pretoria. In 1903 she took ill and on 17 April she died, at the age of sixty-three years. Her obituary which appeared in the *Pretoria News*, was written by Vere Stent, secretary to Cecil John Rhodes.

And so, a tremendously brave and indomitable woman of pioneering spirit lies resting peacefully in the Wesleyan section of the old cemetery in Pretoria. She is an example to us all.

The Po people

In the late 18th century the area around what is now the small town of Magaliesburg, west of Johannesburg in the North West Province, was the ancestral land of the Po people. They are a sub-tribe of the Tswana and their totem is the elephant.

When Mzilikazi fled the wrath of Shaka and entered the Magaliesberg, many, though not all, of the Po fled their lands and migrated down to Thaba Nchu where they lived untroubled by the wrath of the warrior king, who ruled supreme in the Transvaal. When the Voortrekkers arrived, Mzilikazi suspected their intentions and fell upon the Erasmus family near present-day Rustenburg. The scattered Trekkers consolidated in the Parys area and in the Battle of Vegkop that followed, a mere forty families drove back an impi of more than 3 000 Ndebele. The Voortrekkers then attacked and ransacked Mosega, one of Mzilikazi's kraals near Zeerust. At the same time a Zulu impi attacked from the east and, although Mzilikazi himself was safe at eGabeni to the north, his power in the Transvaal was broken. Hendrik Potgieter, the Boer leader, took advantage of this and in a nine-day running battle, Mzilikazi was driven out of the country and up through present-day Botswana to the north, where he went on to form the great Matabele nation.

The Po who had fought alongside the Trekkers against Mzilikazi, then settled in the valley of the Nagakotse (Magalies) River. In 1841 they again fought on the side of the Boers when a group of Ndebele warriors raided into the Transvaal. This, however, did not help the Po. The Boers

129

moved inexorably onto their land. They surveyed and cut it up into farms and the Po had to dig irrigation furrows from the river for them. Anybody who has driven through the Hekpoort Valley will know how fertile the land is. The Po were devastated and deeply resentful of the Boers who had stolen their land. In 1847 their Chief Moghali Moghali (after whom the Magaliesberg range is named) was accused of gunrunning and conspiring with chiefs hostile to the Boers. He was summoned to appear before Commandant Kruger, the father of Paul Kruger. Suspicious of the whites' justice, however, Moghali Moghali left his home with a few followers and fled to Thaba Nchu. Years later he and his people came back to make their peace with the then president of the Transvaal, Marthinus Wessels Pretorius. After negotiations the Boers decided to allocate some land north of the Magaliesberg range to the Po, but the fertile valley between the Witwatersberg and the Magaliesberg was not returned.

The Po were told that they would have to purchase the land from the Transvaal Republic, so Moghali Moghali called the tribal elders together and they decided to send all the able-bodied men down to the Cape Province to find work. They then levied a tax upon the men's earnings and in this way were able, in 1863, to pay the Transvaal Government for the return of a portion of their sacred lands. The Po settled just south of the present-day town of Britz at a place called Tlhogokgolo Mountain or Wolhuterskop.

It was no wonder that, when the Anglo-Boer War broke out, they sided with the British, hoping to retrieve their lands, but that too was in vain and the Po still live at the foot of Wolhuterskop to this day.

Mantatisi – the African Boadicea

his is the tale of Mantatisi, the black Boadicea, a woman who
lends credence to the saying that 'hell hath no fury like a woman
scorned'.

It was early in the 1800s and the tribes in what is now Zululand were
fleeing from the wrath of Shaka. Some of these fugitives were given refuge
by Morotsho, Chief of the Batlokwa, a metalworking people whose home
was on the western side of the Drakensberg.

Among the fugitives was a young man named Motsholi. Unfortunately
for him, he engaged the fancy of Mantatisi, Chief Morotsho's wife and
queen of the Batlokwa tribe. She was absolutely smitten by the young
fugitive, though she had a small problem – her husband!

In 1813 Chief Morotsho died mysteriously and Mantatisi immediately
called upon the fugitive Motsholi to be her consort. Motsholi rejected her,
saying, 'Shall I eat Morotsho's food?' His implication was clear – if he were
to take the place of the chief, would he not run the risk of ending up eating
the poisoned food that Mantatisi had used to rid herself of her husband?

This rejection enraged the bloodthirsty Mantatisi. She called upon her
son, Sikonyela and said to him, 'I want Motsholi's collar!' She was
referring to the brass neckband that Motsholi wore to signify his royal rank
amongst his own people. That band was moulded exactly to the man's neck,
and could not be removed without decapitation. Clearly Mantatisi was
demanding Motsholi's death. Sikonyela carried out his mother's
instructions, and, along with Motsholi's head, presented the collar to

Mantatisi on a platter, echoing the story of John the Baptist and Salome. At this point the rest of the fugitives fell upon the Batlokwa and they had to flee, led by their queen.

Scorned in love, Mantatisi's blood boiled. She proceeded to take it out on the entire world, as she knew it, especially upon the Southern Sotho, Koranna and, eventually, the Tswana peoples.

When the fleeing Batlokwa reached the Lekoa, later known as the Vaal River, in the district of Harrismith, Mantatisi called a halt on the banks of the river. She began to put to good use the knowledge she had gleaned from the fugitives, information she had accumulated from the conversations held with the men during their stay with her tribe.

Mantatisi taught the men to fight in the style of Shaka. In fact, she actually bettered Shaka's tactics in her determination to visit a reign of terror on the land. Her warriors, like Shaka's, fought naked, their bodies were polished jet black. They were adorned with gleaming collars, waistbands and armlets of brass and copper, and upon their heads they wore great plumes of ostrich-feathers. She trained them to grimace furiously, and to clamour like demons.

It was said that Mantatisi had a single eye in the middle of her forehead. The explanation for this probably lies in the fact that forty years later diamonds were discovered in her district, and the 'eye' was probably a large diamond strung on a headband. It was also said that Mantatisi fed her warriors on her own breastmilk. This probably symbolizes the queen instilling courage into her warriors.

From then on Mantatisi's warriors were called the Mantatees and, like Shaka, they went on to destroy tribe after tribe, sweeping up from the Harrismith district into the Transvaal, laying everything bare before them, sparing only the strong for warriors, the beautiful to consort with, and killing all the rest, including the very young. The tribes that could not flee were decimated.

On and on she went, destroying everything before her, conquering until there was nothing left to conquer or destroy, and nothing left to eat. The grain was gone, the cattle were gone, the countryside was left completely bare, and the warriors, with no other sustenance, turned to cannibalism. The

132

Mfecane was under way and when, years later, the Voortrekkers arrived on the Highveld, it is true that they found these vast tracts of land uninhabited, and entire villages laid waste. There were only small pockets of people living as cannibals on the tops of hills and mountains.

It was at this time that Mantatisi, now a power-hungry, ruthless despot, made her fatal error. The Mantatees had penetrated very far west, into the Koranna country, and they fell upon the Koranna, thinking that fighting them would be no different from any other tribe. The Koranna numbered only 150, and the Mantatees 15 000, but the Koranna had firearms and the Mantatees did not. Bullets could reach where spears could not and, using the tactical withdrawal system that had yet to become famous in this country's military history, the Koranna tore the Mantatees to shreds. The Koranna were, to some extent, under the influence of the missionary Robert Moffat, and showed no mercy for these cannibal hordes.

Another tribe in the same area of the Vaal or Lekoa River were the Batlaping, a weak but very cruel tribe, so the missionary notes and diaries inform us. They joined the Griqua in the battle but not until the only warriors left on the field were the wounded and the dead. The Batlaping stoned and speared the wounded remnants of Manatatisi's army. They cut off heads and kicked them about. They severed arms and legs and carried them around as trophies. Not one of the wounded survived that day.

Mantatisi was utterly broken in power and her army totally destroyed. She fled back to the Basutoland area from where she had originally come. It is said that she sought refuge with the first king to unite the Basuto people, Moshweshwe the First. Moshweshwe was a wise leader and, realising that living and carrying the burden of what she had done to her people was a far heavier sentence than death, he gave her and her son, Sikonyela refuge in his country. There she died a lonely old woman, driven to the very edge of insanity because of her deeds.

If you go into the Magaliesberg region today, just before the Olifantsnek dam, on the farm called Olifantskloof, you will find the remnants of a village. Its stone walls are where the 'Bakwena Mmatau' or 'The People of the Lion', once lived peacefully. Its ruins are all that Mantatisi's warriors left, a grim reminder of the fearsome warrior queen.

Sir John Swinburne

T ucked away on the side of the N3 highway, halfway between Johannesburg and Durban, lies the tiny settlement of Swinburne, named after Sir John Swinburne, a relative of the famous English poet, Algernon Charles Swinburne. Although Sir John has been largely forgotten today, he remains an interesting character in the history of our country.

Sir John was the 7th Baronet Swinburne, a title created by Charles II in 1660. In 1831, when he was twenty-nine years old, he succeeded his grandfather and inherited over 30 000 acres in Northumberland. As a young man he joined the Royal Navy and saw active service in the Burmese War of 1852, and the Crimean War, after which he was posted to the Baltic where he served until 1858.

He retired, a naval captain, to his ancestral home Capheaton near Newcastle-on-Tyne and married the daughter of another north-country Baronet, Mary Eleanor Brinckman. For the next fourteen years he lived the life of a country gentleman and followed with interest the adventures of a German explorer, Karl Mauch, who became famous in this country. Mauch was prospecting in the interior, eventually landing up in Mashonaland and Matabeleland in what is now Zimbabwe. Swinburne was absolutely smitten by Mauch's reports of gold in the area called the 'Tati Territory'. This is the area where our Northern Province meets Botswana and Zimbabwe. The find came about in the following manner. A famous elephant hunter, Henry Hartley from Magaliesberg in the

Transvaal (on whom Sir Rider Haggard based the character of Alan Quartermain), on an ivory-hunting expedition to the Zambezi Valley, had stumbled upon ancient gold diggings in Matabeleland. He told the story to Mauch. Mauch was intrigued by the story of the gold diggings that had been worked by an ancient people in a time long gone. But more of that another time.

Several local gold companies were formed. Two of these, one under Captain Black, consisting of thirty-four Australian diggers, and the other under a Mr MacNeil, set out to find the Tati goldfields. Both failed.

Sir John Swinburne, his head full of these tales, met Captain Arthur Lionel Levert in 1868 and between them they formed the London and Limpopo Mining Company. They raised money, purchased plant, hired staff and in the same year landed at Durban. Soon after landing they began their trek into the interior, loaded with all the equipment of a central African expedition: guns, ammunition, traps for wild animals, tents, ropes, shovels, picks, crowbars, cooking utensils and everything else required for a mining operation in the remote bush.

Sir John had also brought along a steam traction engine, the first ever to land in South Africa. He was aiming to introduce mechanised road transport to South Africa. At this time the only railways in South Africa consisted of 2 km of line from Durban Harbour to the Point, 11 km of line from Cape Town to Wynberg and about 60 km of line to Wellington. So the arrival of this 'beast' was quite spectacular. It steamed and snarled its way through that trackless country, bumping over boulders, levelling dongas and cleaving a path through virgin bush. Wherever there was a pan, they would stop to fill the boiler and, from the surrounding bush, fine wood was continually cut to feed this insatiable monster.

Alas, the steam traction engine was way before its time. It never completed the journey. It was abandoned along the way and eventually sold. So, somewhere in Natal lie the ruins of this amazing vehicle, which chuffed ponderously through the bush where only people, horses and ox wagons had gone before.

Swinburne was not to be deterred. The traction engine may have proved unequal to the task imposed on it, but another first for South Africa,

135

was a static steam engine which survived the 500 km trek and arrived in Tati in April 1869. Foundations were laid and the engine was put to work. Mzilikazi, the king of the Matabele, was so impressed by Swinburne that he granted him prospecting rights in what was to become known as the Northern Goldfields. Sir John had a stamp battery designed and made in Durban – another first for South Africa – and had it taken up to the mine by ox-wagon.

By this time other prospectors had reached the area and had established themselves along 'Todd's Creek'. Here a great deal of energy was spent and shafts, up to 150 feet deep were sunk, but the gold values proved patchy. Sir John, ever restless in nature, left August Greite in charge of the mine and set off for Pretoria, where he met the President of the Zuid-Afrikaansche Republiek, Marthinus Wessels Pretorius. Even after a cursory examination of the country, he was convinced that it was highly mineralised and so, in March 1860, he put to President Pretorius a proposal that even today is astonishing in both its foresight and its naivety.

The proposal was, first, that the ZAR grant exclusive rights to the London and Limpopo Company for the running of trackless steam engines throughout the Transvaal and, secondly, that the Company establish banks and manufacturing companies, as well as import goods and machinery, and that it act as sole agents for the ZAR.

To appreciate the situation, one should be aware that at this time the ZAR was totally bankrupt. Sir John knew this and proposed to alleviate the treasury's plight. He offered to redeem the £60 000-worth of 'blue-back' notes the ZAR Government had issued by purchasing them at 10 shillings per £1 and paying as follows: 2 shillings and 6 pence in British coin; 2 shillings and 6 pence in the Company's own notes, payable at six months; and 5 shillings in its own notes, payable at two years. The Company's notes would be payable at its own banks, as well as banks in the Cape and Natal.

In return, the ZAR was to hand over all its lands to the Company as security until the notes had been redeemed and, furthermore, all the mineral rights on land not owned by individuals would be given to the Company in freehold tenure. The Company would also be given exclusive right to grant banking licences and, lastly, would receive a 5% commission from the net proceeds of farms sold.

When the Company had repaid itself, the amount of the outstanding notes – £60 000 as well as the 5% commission – the remaining farms would be returned to the Government, but the mineral rights would remain the property of the London and Limpopo Trading and Mining Company.

Professor Arndt has pointed out that the Company would have made a clear profit of £30 000 on the notes and some £3 000 in commissions. So in reality, it was offering £50 000 for the perpetual ownership of the mineral rights to the Transvaal. What is more amazing was that the offer received the backing of some of the Volksraad! The offer was considered in May 1869 and received careful attention. A technical difficulty arose. Sir John had forgotten to put the Company's Articles of Association in as supporting documentation. Yet, there was some considerable support, as the Transvaal's paper money could not get 2 shillings and 6 pence in hard cash. It is pleasing to note, however, that the ZAR did not sell the Transvaal's mineral rights to Sir John.

When the deal fell through, Sir John had had enough. He returned to England, leaving Captain Levert in charge. The gold proved erratic and in 1872, having sent more that 2 000 ounces of gold to England, the London and Limpopo Trading and Mining Company faded into obscurity and the stamp battery stopped for good.

Other companies were formed, among them Tati Concessions and the Tati Blue Jacket Syndicate, and if today you travel by rail to Zimbabwe via Botswana, just outside Francistown you may still see the ruins of the Settlement of the Monarch Reef.

Sir John Swinburne lived to see the birth of the Rand and the rise of Johannesburg. By the time he died, gold worth more than one thousand million pounds sterling had been recovered in the Transvaal.

Swinburne, the little settlement just near Van Reenen's Pass, proudly bears his name.

The flight of the Herero

Everywhere in the gleaming sands lie the rusted parts of abandoned wagons, trek chains, thongs, and canvas tarpaulins, along with the bones of men and cattle, and the graves of those fallen in the most grievous of deaths – thirst. For a trekker, there was no word that could instil greater fear than *dors* (thirst) – the stories of the Dorsland treks live to this very day. Those who experienced a 'small thirst' on one of those treks never forgot the experience. The continual groaning of the oxen is the most heartrending sound that could ever come from an animal. Added to this was the blazing heat of the sun, the endless sand and the choking cloud of dust as they trekked onwards, becoming thirstier and thirstier.

One such Dorsland trek has attracted very little attention in our country, probably because it was a black trek. The old newspaper *Die Brandwag* published the story in 1921.

It was the trek of the Herero out of South West Africa which went eastwards through the Kalahari and into the country of the Bamangwato, eventually coming to an end in Phalala, in the Waterberg region of what is now the North-West Province of South Africa. The size of this disastrous trek was unbelievable. More than 700 wagons were left behind in the desert, and more than 13 000 people died of thirst, the most terrible of all deaths.

The ovaHerero tribe originated in Central Africa and its people are exceptionally tall – an adult under 1,8 m is very unusual. At the time of this little-known trek, the majority of the tribe was educated and could read and write. High Dutch was their daily language. They built houses, wore European clothing and farmed, and were generally known to be a friendly people. It was said that their attitudes changed with the colonisation by the Germans, that they were influenced by the yellow people, and turned to murdering whites. I have heard this all too often in the stories of the Gqunukhwebe, the Xhosa and the Koranna at Mamusa, the list is endless. Behind the myth lies the greed to occupy land, and it was no different in the case of the Germans in South West Africa.

The Bondelswart Hottentots put up a fight on the plains surrounding the Karas Mountains and, when the Herero saw what happened to them, they were so shattered that the only option they could think of was flight. 'Rather face the Kalahari', said the elders of the tribe, 'than face the Germans'.

So they prepared themselves for the long trek, before the German forces even reached their boundaries. They sent intelligence parties out to gather information about grazing, waterholes, Tsamma melons and general conditions, but nothing could have prepared them for the ordeal that they were about to face. The trek started and the Germans, following them to the last waterhole, reported that, even at this stage, they were following a path of dead and dying people and animals. Every waterhole was filled with dead cattle and the water trampled to mud. It is estimated that 4 000 Herero died, even before the big thirst began. The head of the trek was under Captain Samuel and the rearguard under one Julius, a preacher and schoolteacher.

When they left their homes there were more than 700 wagons, 14 000 people and cattle uncountable, but upon arrival in the Waterberg there were but 400 people and no animals except for a horse belonging to Samuel and the cattle given to them by the kindly people of Khama, the Bamangwato. It is estimated that in the desert 3 600 people died of thirst alone. There were very few old people or children that came through that crossing, and seldom has nature imposed her harsh code of 'survival of the fittest' more cruelly upon a people. Contrary to the hopelessly optimistic reports of the scouts, there were was very little grazing to be had, the pan water was scarce and the Tsamma melons were green and bitter to the taste. Three days after entering the desert, the cattle began to die, and what made matters worse was the panicky knowledge that the Germans were after them. All the known waterholes were rushed by thousands of thirsty cattle and immediately churned into mud, so the cattle were unable to relieve their thirst.

Inevitably, within fourteen days the last of the 700 wagons had to be abandoned. Everything transportable was made into bundles and everyone, young and old, had to help carry. In the forefront was Samuel, trying desperately to keep order. At the back was Julius, making sure that the weak and frail were not left behind. On the flanks, daily, were patrols to collect Tsamma melons, which would be distributed among all the people. It took a lot of melons to keep the people going, of course, so, as much meat as could be carried, was made into biltong. But it soon became apparent that strict order could not be maintained and, within a week or two, the trek was so long and extended that the stragglers took fully three days to arrive at the place where the forward group had camped. Under these circumstances, of course, no fair sharing of meat and melons was possible. Contrary to what one would expect, there was very little selfishness, and heroic acts abounded.

The first to fall were the elderly and, almost every day, the rear section of the trek would pass small groups of them, usually lying under the shade of a thorn tree, having made their peace with God, and simply waiting to die. Usually the goodbyes and a little prayer had been said, and those who were strong enough moved on with the trek. Where a person had died in the company of another family member, he or she would be buried up to his or her neck in the sand. Mothers with suckling babies bore the brunt of the pain and very few made it through. 'You could count them on your fingers', Julius said.

The unfortunate mothers with more than one child had an even worse time of it, and often you would see a mother walk the path three times, as she carried her children forward one by one, along the trek and, sooner or later, these poor mothers came to realise that one, or even two would have to be sacrificed, to save the last one. Many mothers actually had the courage to kill their children, instead of leaving them to a lingering death in the blazing sun. Samuel and Julius agreed – there was no option – though usually this decision was taken far too late and most of the mothers died shortly thereafter. One young woman, Maria, who gave birth to her first child at the beginning of the trek, used a galvanized iron bathtub as a sled and pulled her baby through the desert – and made it. Unfortunately, when a suckling mother becomes dehydrated, her milk dries up. Many babies died of hunger, usually shortly followed by the mother who would inflict knife wounds to her breasts in a vain attempt to give sustenance to the dying child. Julius recalled an elderly couple, long married – the woman was too weak and could go no further. The man was strong and would have pulled through, but decided to stay with his wife in the desert. They bade farewell to their children, their bundles were redistributed and the trek moved on, with the vultures always circling overhead.

The survivors went on, with feet and legs swollen, without skin, and bleeding. Their lips and tongues swelled up and cracked, so much so that it was almost impossible to eat the Tsamma melons. For two months they had not seen water.

Suddenly, these skeletons dressed in rags, heard voices calling them, but, with their burnt lips and burst tongues, all they could manage in answer was a hiss, as the Bamangwato tribe of Khama came into the desert to save them. Slowly, oh so slowly, the Bamangwato nursed the survivors back from the brink. Water was given in half measures to the weakest and the children first, then the others and, to those nearest to death, it was administered drop by drop, for drinking would have killed them.

After six months' recuperation, the remnants of the Herero tribe moved on to Phalala in the Waterberg, where this terrible, but largely forgotten epic was recorded, and is still spoken about very softly at night, around the fires.

The search for Utopia

B etween the Nahoon and Konyhana rivers in the Eastern Cape lies Africa's real life Utopia, in which the poet laureate, Alfred Lord Tennyson, played a part. The colony was named after him – Tennysonia.

The story starts with the death of General Gordon in Khartoum. On the crest of the great wave of emotion that passed through England, 'The Gordon Memorial League' was established to perpetuate the qualities of religious faith, idealism and military genius. The purpose of the League was to train poor, unemployed people in English towns to enable them to go farming in South Africa. Gordon and Tennyson had often discussed this idea.

Every man was to be given between 20 and 50 acres of land, 10 head of cattle and 10 sheep. There would be no charge for the first year and a subsistence allowance would be paid for six months. After a year a charge of £10 per family per year would be levied until £200 had been repaid. Huts, tools, implements, wagons and seed were all provided free of charge, and only families were sent out because of the isolation.

The League set up in King William's Town and 3 400 acres were purchased from the Carnarvon Estate. In August 1886 twenty-four families arrived at East London and trekked to the pleasant hilly country of Tennysonia. There they found huts fitted out with stoves and furniture, even groceries had been delivered and the League had provided a schoolroom with a teacher.

142

In 1887 Alfred White, one of the founders of the Gordon Memorial Trust, came out to South Africa to report on the progress of the scheme and found nothing but discontent amongst the settlers. The huts were too small, the plots were too small, and the produce prices were too low. White realised that it had been a mistake to select settlers who were not farmers and recommended that those who did not wish to stay be entitled to leave the land and be replaced with more suitable families of farming stock. Part of the problem was that the goldfields of the Witwatersrand had been discovered and this proved an irresistible drawcard to the settlers, who all wanted to trek to Johannesburg.

In June 1888, 25 families from Hampshire arrived and joined the remaining 13 families in Tennysonia. Each of the 25 new cottages had a fenced garden and 50 acres of arable land, 33 acres of ordinary soil and 13 acres of very rich, black vlei soil.

The lands, planted with potatoes, were expected to yield some 6 000 bags. Large fields of mealies and forage were planted. A little over nine megalitres of water was earmarked for irrigation per day, after it had passed over the water-wheel that drove the flourmill. Dams holding 910 megalitres of water were constructed to serve, among other things, the strawberry beds and orchards. More than 2 000 oaks, as well as other trees, were planted. The flourmill cost £8 000 and was powered by a 10 m waterfall driving a turbine that produced 22 kW.

Most of the settlers, whose names are still familiar in the Eastern Cape, such as Cock, Marshall, Wyatt, Baker, Cranmer, Mountsford, Pressley, Griffiths, Bolton, Godfrey and Watts, stayed on. Some of them moved to the highlands of the then British Kaffraria and others to the goldfields.

Alfred White, after this second try, realised that Utopia was not be be attained this way – but let's face it, it was an honest and gallant attempt.

The First
Frontier War

T he Eastern Cape area has a history that would take a lifetime to
understand, reconstruct and rewrite, because most of the accounts
are very one-sided and jingoed in favour of the Dutch, the British,
and the settlers themselves. Now it is time to tell the other side of the
story. For those who would like to read a balanced and accessible
account of those troubled times between the 1770s and 1880s, Noel
Mostert's magnificent book, *Frontiers,* published in 1992, is a must.

There are memorable figures from that time, such as Coenraad de
Buys, Willem Prinsloo and many others, but we will keep them for
another story. We will turn our attention now to the actual causes of the
First Frontier War and its final outcome. In the 1770s the Dutch East
India Company found itself compelled to proclaim formal boundaries
beyond which the trekboers could not go – this after a period of
expansion with half-hearted attempts at control by threats and warnings.
Previously there had been no formally defined Eastern Frontier. Now
firm limits were imposed. This was delineated at Bruintjieshoogte in the
North and the Gamtoos River in the West, just on the Cape side of Algoa
Bay, near present-day Jeffreys Bay. Some trekboers had settled, or were
looking to settle, beyond those markers and one of the first Afrikaaner
families to become distinctly recognisable in this regard were the
Prinsloos. They did not come rougher or tougher than that family.
Willem Prinsloo, an elephant hunter and cattle trader, was the principal
boundary breaker and bounty hunter. When the Cape authorities sought

runaway slaves or military deserters, it was Prinsloo who would offer to bring them back – for a consideration, of course. The Prinsloo family has now almost faded into the mists of time, but at that stage, for almost sixty years, they were at the centre of most frontier mischief, and were eventually directly accused of being responsible for starting the First Frontier War between the Xhosa and the Colonists. Finally, in 1815, we see Prinsloo, together with some others, hanging by the neck – the first Afrikaner martyrs to the British. This botched execution was used to whip up nationalism in the 1948 election. The Afrikaners never forgot Slagtersnek.

The story unfolds thus. At the beginning of the 1770s we find the first records of old Willem Prinsloo, moving out beyond Bruintjieshoogte, between Graaff-Reinet and Somerset East, into the land and the pastures of the Xhosa. This led to his family's fateful place in our country's history. By 1772, he had established himself on two farms in the Fish River Valley. The authorities ordered him to return, because he was outside the boundary, but instead Prinsloo was joined by thirteen other trekboers, who all petitioned the Cape for permission to remain there. In 1775 the authorities granted the request and then arbitrarily drew new boundaries, this time the Fish River to the East of Bruintjieshoogte and the Bushman's River near the coast. This appears to have been done by decree, with no consultation with the Xhosa Chiefs at all. The Chiefs were most unhappy with the situation as they were being pushed westwards by Chief Rarabe, who demanded the submission of outlying chiefdoms, such as those of Gwali, Mdange and Ntinde.

This is how the first of the most crucial relationships on that frontier started off – an interpenetration of two distinct societies, one indigenous and the other intrusive. The history of the region as a frontier 'opens' when the first members of the intrusive society arrive and 'closes' when a single political authority takes control of the area.

The Prinsloos were said to have staged a cattle raid on the Xhosa in which a Prinsloo lost his life. The Xhosa retaliated by raiding the Boers. The actual official account gives the benefit of doubt to the Xhosa, blaming the Prinsloos outright for being mischievous inhabitants, who would resort to any knavery to have the local blacks removed, in order to enlarge their own farms.

A commando was sent out, and in its report one can see the very seeds of the dilemma facing South Africa, then and in the future. Written on 13 March 1780, it is a masterpiece:

'Upon the proceedings of this commando, as it appears to me, will depend the doubtful question as to whether the Xhosa are to be forcibly dislodged, or the inhabitants obliged to abandon that part of the Country.'

This commando, under Adriaan van Jaarsveld, was told to drive the Xhosa back over the Fish River, with such force as was deemed necessary. As for the Bushmen, 'There being no hope of peace, you are at liberty to put them to death, and entirely destroy them.'

The commando engaged the Xhosa, and Van Jaarsveld arranged his men so as to be able to shoot to the front and the back. He told them to dismount, then collected all the chewing tobacco that his men had in their possession and cut it into small pieces. He then walked forward to confront the Xhosa, threw the tobacco at them and as they came forward to pick it up, Prinsloo gave the order to open fire.

This ended the first major conflict in that area, which was, in my humble opinion, one of the root causes of the eight frontier wars that followed, just as one of the root causes of the Second World War was actually the harsh terms imposed on Germany by the peace treaty that ended the First World War! Do we never learn?

The story of Maria Oosthuizen

During the Anglo-Boer War there lived in the eastern Free State near the town of Zastron, a young woman named Maria, whose farmer husband was away on commando. Maria and her maid Sabina were living alone when they heard of the impending arrival of the British troops, coming to burn their farm. They took refuge in a freshly dug pit under some corrugated iron and remained there until the conflagration had passed and night had fallen. Under the cover of night, they ran for the Maluti Mountains.

At daybreak a British search party scoured the area and it is said that a Scottish soldier found them hiding in a cave. Maria begged him to leave them alone and he turned around, walked out of the cave and reported that it was empty. Thus they made good their escape into Lesotho and eventually arrived in the small town of Matatiele.

Maria, with help of Sabina who was a trained inyanga, started to eke out a living by curing illnesses with natural herbs and medicines, and soon became renowned for her healing powers. Sadly, it was at this time that she learnt that her husband had been killed while fighting in the war.

The local Dutch Reformed Church (NGK) Minister in Matatiele, Dominee Oosthuizen, preached against her from the pulpit, declaring that her cures were unnatural and the work of the devil, and that the people must cease consulting her. Then, when he himself fell ill and was tended by her and nursed back to health, he fell in love with her and they were married.

Shortly after this, Oosthuizen was transferred to the district of Greytown in Natal, to preach amongst the Zulus. One Friday evening in 1918 he came back from visiting an outlying district and fell from his horse, desperately ill. He told Maria that the Zulus were dying in their hundreds from an unknown disease, and he himself died the following day.

Maria retired to her room and scoured her books to seek a cure. After three days she mounted her horse and rode off into Zululand. From kraal to kraal she rode, telling the Chiefs to instruct their people to drink their own urine as an antidote to the illness. So great was her name amongst the Zulu people that nobody questioned her. And so it was that the Zulu nation was saved from the tragic influenza pandemic that killed so many millions of people during the years 1918 to 1919. However, Maria was so devastated by her husband's death that she sold the farm and moved to Johannesburg, still accompanied by the faithful Sabina.

In her old age she wrote how bitterly disappointed she was that Sabina had deserted her in her time of need. What she did not know was that Sabina had walked all the way back to Zululand and had informed the Chiefs that the old woman was dying. An impi was despatched at once to bring Maria back to Zululand. They arrived in Johannesburg but her door at the boarding house was locked. They broke it down and found her there, lying dead in her bed.

That impi gently gathered up the body of the old woman and carried her all the way back to Zululand. The Chiefs, at the direct orders of the King, gave her a royal Zulu burial in eMakhosini, also known as the Place of Kings. So it is there that the mortal remains of a brave Afrikaans woman, who won the undying respect of that proud people, lies buried in the place most sacred to the Zulus.

The Adelaide Dutch Reformed Church

delaide, a small, restful village in the Eastern Cape, not far from Somerset East, came into existence as a military outpost during the Frontier Wars against the Xhosa and Pondo during the middle of the 19th century. It remained a sleepy, delightful little sheep-farming hamlet and was eventually occupied by the British forces during the Anglo-Boer War of 1899–1902.

During their occupation of Adelaide, the British commandeered the local Dutch Reformed Church and converted it into barracks for their men. The Rectory they converted into stables. This did not go down too well with the local Afrikaans townsfolk, but there was nothing much they could do for, as is customary in such times, the occupying forces had scant regard for the property and possessions of the Adelaide townsfolk.

After the war and the withdrawal of the troops, the local community wished to restore their place of worship. Throughout South Africa, however, there was a dire shortage of money. Everyone in Adelaide was willing to lend a hand and donate their labour, but there were no funds to buy the materials essential for the restoration.

Then a strange thing happened. Three months after the failed restoration donation drive, into the town came two long-wheelbase transport or commissariat wagons. They were piled high with fine cut timber, along with a beautifully hand-carved pulpit and matching chair. The congregation were astounded! They immediately withdrew some of the nastier names that they had found for the British officers and troops during the occupation of their beloved town. They now realised that the British people had a conscience and had sent the timber all the way from England as an apology.

The delighted members of the congregation immediately set to work and within a few months, the restored church and rectory was proudly standing. It looked spectacular and the people settled down to their normal Sunday routine.

A few years later, a letter addressed to the Mayor of Adelaide arrived. It said:

To: The Honourable Mayor, Adelaide, South Africa
From: The Mayor of Adelaide, Australia

Dear Sir,
It is with some trepidation that we enquire as to whether a consignment of oak wood, which we ordered from England about two years ago for our new church, has not, perhaps, by mistake been delivered to your town in South Africa instead of ours.

Well, there was not much that the town council could do, the restoration was complete. Instead they had photographs taken of the beautiful new interior of their church and sent them off to the Mayor of Adelaide, Australia, together with an explanatory letter telling of how the British had commandeered their church during the war.

And that is how the interior of the church was restored and still stands today, a monument to a lovely mistake.

Bibliography

Aylward, A. 1878. *The Transvaal of Today*. W. Blackwood & Sons, London.

Becker, Peter. 1967. *The Path of Blood*. Longman, London.

Becker, Peter. 1969. *Hill of Destiny*. Longman, London.

Becker, Peter. 1970. *Rule of Fear*. Longman, London.

Blackburn, Douglas. 1908. *The Prinsloo of Prinsloosdorp*. Alston Rivers, London.

Binns, C.T. 1974. *The Warrior People*. Howard B. Timmins, Cape Town.

Bloomhill, Greta. 1962. *Witchcraft in Africa*. Howard B. Timmins, Cape Town.

Bulpin, Tom. V. 1952. *Shaka's Country*. Howard B. Timmins, Cape Town.

Bulpin, Tom. V. 1953. *The Golden Republic*. Howard B. Timmins, Cape Town.

Bulpin, Tom. V. 1954. *To the Shores of Natal*. Howard B. Timmins, Cape Town.

Bulpin, Tom. V. 1955. *Storms over the Transvaal*. Howard B. Timmins, Cape Town.

Bulpin, Tom. V. 1957. *Lost Trails of the Transvaal*. Howard B. Timmins, Cape Town.

Bulpin, Tom. V. 1957. *Islands in a Forgotten Sea*. Howard B. Timmins, Cape Town.

Bulpin, Tom. V. 1959. *Trail of the Copper King*. Howard B. Timmins, Cape Town.

Bulpin, Tom. V. 1966. *Natal and Zulu Country*. Books of Africa, Cape Town.

Carruthers, Vincent. 1990. *The Magaliesburg*. Protea Book House, Pretoria.

Churchill, Lord R. 1994. *Men, Mines & Animals in South Africa*. Books of Rhodesia, Bulawayo

Cope, John. 1967. *The King of the Hottentots*. Howard B. Timmins, Cape Town.

Cloete, Stuart. 1963. *Rags of Glory*. Collins, London.

Cloete, Stuart. 1969. *African Portraits*. Constantia Publications, Cape Town.

Conan Doyle, A. 1903. *The Great Boer War*. Thomas Nielson & Sons. London.

Green, Lawrence G. 1932. *The Coast of Treasure*. Howard B. Timmins, Cape Town.

Green, Lawrence G. 1945. *Where Men Still Dream*. Howard B. Timmins, Cape Town.

Green, Lawrence G. 1949. *Land in the Afternoon*. Howard B. Timmins, Cape Town.

Green, Lawrence G. 1952. *Lords of the Last Frontier*. Howard B. Timmins, Cape Town.

Green, Lawrence G. 1959. *To the River's End*. Howard B. Timmins, Cape Town.

Green, Lawrence G. 1961. *The Great North Road*. Howard B. Timmins, Cape Town.

Green, Lawrence G. 1966. *Thunder on the Blaauberg*. Howard B. Timmins, Cape Town.

Harrington, A.L. 1980. *Sir Harry Smith*. Tafelberg Publishers, Cape Town.

Isaacs, Nathaniel. 1971. *Travels and Adventures*. Killie Campbell, Durban.

Johnson, Frank. 1940. *Great Days*. Books of Rhodesia, Bulawayo.

Klein, Harry. 1951. *Land of the Silver Mists*. Howard B. Timmins, Cape Town.

Kruger, Rayne. 1959. *Goodbye Dolly Gray*. Cassell, London.

Lehman, Joseph. 1972. *The First Boer War*. Jonathan Cape, London.

Lowe, S. 1967. *The Hungry Veld*. Shuter & Shooter, Pietermaritzburg.

Mackeurtan, Graham. 1930. *Cradle Days of Natal*. Longman Green & Co. London.

Manfred, N.H. 1960. *Voortrekkers of South Africa*. Tafelberg Publishers, Cape Town.

Marais, Eugene. 1928. *Sketse uit die Lewe van Mens en Diere*. Nasionale Pers, Cape Town.

McNeile, Michael. 1958. *More True Stories from this Africa*. McAlan, Cape Town.

Metrowich, Frank. 1953. *Assegai over the Hills*. Howard B. Timmins, Cape Town.

Metrowich, Frank. 1962. *Scotty Smith*. Books of Africa, Cape Town.

Milne, Robin. 2000. *Anecdotes of the Anglo Boer War*. Covos Day, Johannesburg.

Morris, David. 1966. *The Washing of the Spears*. Sphere Books, London.

Morton, Henry. 1948. *In Search of South Africa*. Methuen & Co. London.

Mostert, Noel. 1992. *Frontiers*. Pimlico, Johannesburg.

Packenham, Thomas. 1982. *The Boer War*. Futura, London.

Plaatje, Solomon. 1973. *The Boer War Diary*. Macmillan, Johannesburg.

Pringle, Eric. 1963. *Mankazana*. Eric Pringle, East London.

Rosenthal, Eric. 1951. *The Hinges Creaked*. Howard B. Timmins, Cape Town.

Rosenthal, Eric. 1955. *Cutlass and Yardarm*. Howard B. Timmins, Cape Town.

Rosenthal, Eric. 1958. *Other Men's Millions*. Howard B. Timmins, Cape Town.

Rosenthal, Eric. 1959. *Shovel and Sieve*. Howard B. Timmins, Cape Town.

Rosenthal, Eric. 1961. *Encyclopaedia of South Africa*. Frederick Warne, London.

Rosenthal, Eric. 1979. *Memories and Sketches*. AD Donker, London.

Russell, R. 1911. *Natal, the Land and its Story*. D. Dries & Sons, Pietermaritzburg.

Samuelson, R.C. 1974. *Long Long Ago*. T.W. Griggs, Durban.

Scoble, John & Abercrombie, H.R. 1900. *The Rise and Fall of Krugerism*. W. Heinemann, London.

Wannenbergh, Alf. *Forgotten Frontiers*. Howard B. Timmins, Cape Town.

Williams, Alpheos F. 1948. *Some Dreams Come True*. Howard B. Timmins, Cape Town.

Wilson, David M. 1901. *Behind the Scenes in the Transvaal*. Cassell, London.

Wulfson, Lionel. 1987. *Rustenburg at War*. L. Wulfson, Rustenburg.